DATE DUE

GAYLORD

D1053266

Why Conservation Is Failing
and How It Can Regain Ground

ERIC T. FREYFOGLE

Why Conservation Is Failing and How It Can Regain Ground

yale university press   new haven and london

Set in type by SPI Publisher Services.
Printed in the United States of America.

Library of Congress Cataloging-in-Publication Data

Freyfogle, Eric T.
    Why conservation is failing and how it can regain ground/Eric T.
Freyfogle.
        p. cm.
    Includes bibliographical references.
    ISBN-13: 978-0-300-11040-1 (alk. paper)
    ISBN-10: 0-300-11040-5
    1. Conservation of natural resources. I. Title.
S928. F74 2006
333. 72—dc22
                                                        2005023411

A catalogue record for this book is available from
the British Library.

The paper in this book meets the guidelines for
permanence and durability of the Committee on
Production Guidelines for Book Longevity of the
Council on Library Resources.

10 9 8 7 6 5 4 3 2 1

For Donald Worster

What the student (and teacher!) now needs is a text which cuts at right angles to these arbitrary divisions of the land problem; a text which describes the common mechanism of soils, waters, plants and animals as one integral whole; a text which treats of farms, forests, ranges and parks not as different resources, but as different uses of a single resource, the properties of which are first described as a single system, and then traced in their various land-use manifestations.

—Aldo Leopold, 1940

For, alas, the Ideal always has to grow in the Real, and to seek out its bed and board there, often in a very sorry way.

—Thomas Carlyle, 1843

Contents

Introduction

Participants in today's clashes regarding land conservation—using *land* in its broadest ecological sense, to include not just soils but wildlife, water, ecological processes, *and* humans—tend to approach the battlegrounds from two quite different directions. Those who promote conservation typically respond to some inner longing to respect nature's processes. They care about living creatures, often passionately, and want nature's beauties and life forms near at hand. On their side, critics of conservation are prone to approach the issue from a felt need to protect individual liberty. They value the free exercise of entrepreneurial energies and prefer government to remain at bay. What neither side seems to deem necessary, as they debate and spar, is to consider conservation as a serious body of cultural and political thought.

Conservation advocates largely view this task as unnecessary. For them, a love of nature and the urge to conserve it provide sufficient motive and guidance for their work. Persistent critics of conservation avoid the task because it is unhelpful to them—and because, practically speaking, they can get away with it. It is easier to criticize conservation's ill-considered fringe than it is to seek out and evaluate its intellectual core. Intellectual atrophy has been one result of this inattention. Fragmented and ineffective conservation has been another.

The conservation cause is under siege today in large part because the public has become confused about what it is trying to do and at what cost. As critics see it, land conservation is about protecting nature from people. It is driven by a wilderness ideal in which humans inevitably bring about degradation. Worse than that, according to critics, laws restricting development trample on private property rights, constrain liberty, and inhibit economic growth. Given these complaints—which are plausible enough on the surface—is it any wonder that conservation efforts have stalled?

A century ago, conservation's main stem had a clear, publicly understood goal. It was to promote the efficient, productive management of natural resources—those parts of nature that were directly useful to people.[1] That practical work has now largely passed to organized commercial interests such as Monsanto, Con-Agra, and Weyerhauser Paper. When conservationists today talk about resource flows it's usually about the harms caused by their production and about such resource uses as recreation and wildlife protection, not about food, heat, and shelter. Conservation, so it appears, is about optional amenities rather than bread-and-butter basics. Laws protecting air and drinking water address essential human needs. But what about measures that preserve wildlands, free-flowing rivers, and rare species? How do they help people? How do they align with the values and dreams of ordinary Americans?

The conservation cause, I believe, is stymied less because of its disciplined opponents than because it lacks good overall direction. And it lacks this because it isn't taking time to stand back—from its work, from society, and from the sweep of history—to think deeply about the larger questions. It is failing to attend seriously to its intellectual and ethical foundations and to ensure that its work and rhetoric build upon them. It isn't considering how land conservation fits into America's self-image as the land of opportunity and progress. If the conservation cause doesn't take its own ideas seriously—and by many measures it doesn't—why should anyone else? Good intentions, good values, even high energy are not enough in themselves.[2]

When taken seriously, as a vital strand of political and cultural thought, conservation poses a forceful challenge to elements of modern culture accepted as fundamental. It questions not merely specific land-use practices but our entrenched ways of seeing and valuing nature. It challenges our excessive faith in science and the capitalist market along with our exaggerated emphasis on individual autonomy. By situating humans within a value-infused natural order, the cause overlaps with religious traditions that honor the Creation. By emphasizing connections among people and between people and land, it promotes a community-centered perspective of life that contrasts with social views exalting individualism. In its call for citizens to broaden their moral and aesthetic sensibilities, it fits within America's long heritage of progressive social reform.

Conservation's intellectual core and intellectual leaders draw little attention save in the pages of academic journals. The public scarcely hears of them or from them. Among the thoughtful leaders are our environmental historians, who have been quietly telling us for years that land degradation is caused less by material factors—such as population, technology, and fossil fuel use—than by our outdated cultural values and assumptions, particularly our ingrained tendency to treat nature as a warehouse of market commodities.[3] To succeed, conservation has to confront these cultural flaws and do so in ways that are orchestrated and deliberate, not haphazard and indirect.

Paradoxically, one sign of conservation's current malaise is supplied by the strand of the movement that has flourished the most of late: the tract-by-tract preservation work performed by the Nature Conservancy, the Trust for Public Land, and hundreds of local land trusts.[4] These groups protect valuable land parcels; their efforts, by and large, are useful. But piecemeal conservation work can come at high cost when it is not thoughtfully situated in a broader, grounded vision of people living harmoniously in an interconnected land. It can cause problems when it is not part of a well-considered challenge to business as usual in America.

Out in the field, tract-by-tract work competes for dollars and support with other conservation efforts. When its practitioners focus only on specific parcels, not on larger landscapes, they inevitably weaken conservation's emphasis on ecological interdependence. Unless particularly careful in word and deed, they can also muddle the movement's cultural criticisms, especially of free market capitalism and of our excessive individualism. We might consider, as a leading example of this conflict, the challenge of promoting conservation on privately owned lands. When one element of the conservation cause pays landowners to conserve (by buying easements or development rights or by endorsing government payment programs), how can another element contend that good land use ought to be a minimum obligation of citizen-owners, enforceable by legal sticks rather than financial carrots?

In the flush of successfully protecting the individual parcel, it has become too easy to forget about the larger landscape, about the plight of taxpayers, and about the unceasing, econo-techno-juggernaut that land-trust work often diverts but never really slows.

Perhaps the most damning evidence of conservation's current plight is the public's tendency to label it a "liberal" cause. Categorized as such, conservation is viewed suspiciously by religious and conservative elements of society through a form of guilt-by-association reasoning. The schism is as dismaying as it is unnecessary. And it has arisen, just as other problems have, because conservation's intellectual core has become lost to the public view. In ways that religious conservatives could come to applaud, conservation's leading voices bemoan public irresponsibility, eroding senses of community, and capitalism's assault on cultural values. No cause takes more seriously the call to respect God's Creation. Conservation is about living a responsible, moral life; about caring for neighbors and children; about vesting moral worth in future generations.

So long as conservation lacks an encompassing ecological vision, the public is unlikely to see how protecting nature's parts helps the larger integrated whole. And so long as the cause represses its criticisms of market capitalism and self-centered behavior, conservationists are unlikely to forge working alliances with other social reformers.

Conservation's critics have deliberately heightened the divide between conservation and moral conservatism by unfairly labeling the cause as elitist or misanthropic. Yet, conservationists have added to their own woes. In the day-to-day flurry we've lost track of our central values and visions. We've become too content to work within the system instead of pushing for change. By settling for small victories and trying to appear more "reasonable," we have not simply pulled back from the larger fight but confused the public about the kind of healthy, vibrant world we want to bring about. In the name of liberal inclusiveness, many conservation groups now honor a multiplicity of voices. But multiple voices should be the input, not the public output. When conservation speaks with multiple voices, the results inevitably are fragmentation, public confusion, and a compromised ability to deflect critics.

When it first gained steam a century ago, organized conservation was less liberal than society as a whole. Classical liberalism honors individuals as such, respecting their free choices, liberating them from constraints, and using government to level the playing field. Conservation, instead, was about holding individuals accountable, about standing up for communities under assault from the wasteful excesses of freewheeling business. It was a reaction against individualism that had gone too far.[5]

These days, the cause appears in a much different

light, at least to outsiders. Conservation is viewed as using government to interfere with private life rather than to protect families and communities. It comes across as antibusiness and antigrowth, not procommunity and promorality. When a group such as the Nature Conservancy enters the market to buy land, grabbing tracts away from waiting developers, it can appear as merely another market participant with its own special (albeit altruistic) aims. Because land parcels set aside for conservation so rarely provide food or shelter, the cause seems to ignore basic human needs. It is easily accused of fostering elitist aims through meddlesome means.

Is it any wonder that the public resists, despite its fondness for nature and its worries about where we're heading in our treatment of it?

This book is a plea to fellow conservationists to take our cause more seriously in intellectual and moral terms. It is a call for us collectively to stand back and think intently about our overarching aims, what it will take to accomplish them, and how we can best communicate them. It is also an appeal to think big in terms of how we might effect social and cultural change, not merely be content with rearguard victories. As for readers who are not committed conservationists, my aim is to describe the landscape, intellectually and morally, and to identify the most promising paths.

Chapter 1 considers the cultural wars now raging in America. Conservationists have been drawn into them—and we're not fighting very well. I take as my point of departure an essay by Wendell Berry, in which he divides society into two factions: the pro-conservation party of "the local community" and the opposing, ascendant party of "the global economy." It's a useful dichotomy, but perhaps not as accurate as another one: that between the supporters of communities of all sizes and those who exalt ardent individualism and the unfettered market. Conservation is being successfully attacked by claims that it clashes with key cultural values, liberty and private property most of all. We require a far more thoughtful, coherent defense on these issues.

Sound intellectual work is particularly needed in engaging with the capitalist market, which is at once a powerful engine of economic creation and the main cause of declining lands. We urgently need a probing study of the market, identifying its strengths and weaknesses. Given the market's preeminent role in shaping landscapes, it is shocking how little we understand about its workings. Conservationists could help in this task. What does the market do well, what does it do poorly, and what constraints should we impose upon it?

Though my comments here are mostly meant to chide conservation's faults as a working reform effort—to issue a plea to leaders and activists—the academy is not without its own shortcomings. On this problem I turn to the literature in my own academic field, environmental law, outlining in chapter 2 how scholarly writing so often conceals its underlying cultural assumptions. Normative views on environmental law differ sharply, with policy recommendations that openly clash. Yet, the true disagreements among scholars mostly reside well beneath the surface, in the undiscussed but influential values that scholars carry with them to their opening pages. Conservation needs to identify and confront these assumptions, which are too often ill considered and miscast. A steady stream of sunlight could clear away some fog. Environmental law is merely one of many relevant academic fields, but it is in the legal arena where so many cultural battles take place and policy choices are made. In this setting, perhaps more than any other, we need to identify clearly what is at stake.

Chapter 3 turns to one of the disturbing trends in conservation today: its tendency, in an effort to appear more accommodating, to water down its criticisms and landscape visions into some variant of merely being-nice-to-nature. Here my point of departure is Michael Pollan's engaging meditation on humans and the garden, *Second Nature*. As a guiding light, I contend, Pollan's prominent book is evocative but distinctly unsatisfying. It represents an across-the-board retreat from where conservation has been and ought to be. Its popularity despite its deficiencies (and that of similar writings) carries troubling implications.

Chapter 4 digs into what passes as the heart of conservation for many people, the idea of sustainability. As an overall goal, I suggest, sustainability is sorely lacking, and not merely because it is so vague about *what* is being sustained (a frequent complaint). To rally around sustainability is to turn our backs on a good many conservation lessons accumulated over the past century at high cost. Merely to catalogue the leading lessons of the past century—a worthwhile task, for those who haven't done it—is to see how vacuous sustainability really is. As a guiding vision sustainability is uninspiring and blurred; its popularity a sign of intellectual amnesia. We can do far better.

Chapter 5 shifts gears, moving from firm but friendly criticism to the task of reconstruction. If conservation is not about sustainability, what, then, is its purpose? To address that question, I turn to the challenge of land management, trying to determine what constitutes good land use. The relevant factors, it turns out, are many, and as we dissect them the subject becomes increasingly complex. Once the pieces are teased apart and labeled, it is possible to isolate the role that science properly plays and to specify how utility, ethics, aesthetics, and human ignorance all fit into the mix. To take an all-things-considered look at good land use is to see how intellectually demanding conservation really is. It is also to see why well-considered strategies and aims, linked to cultural change, are essential.

In chapter 6 I propose six core tasks for the conservation cause to address, starting with the call for a clearer overall goal. I conclude, looking ahead, with "A Conservation Message to the American People."

At the end of the book is an annotated bibliography of writings on conservation's critique of modern culture. My reading recommendations, inevitably idiosyncratic, center around twelve books by leading conservation voices. To engage with these books is to perceive in a whole new light not only land conservation but America's history and culture. The conservation cause does have good ideas and serious minds. We need to use them with greater deliberation and with greater courage.

Early in the book I draw on the writings of two twentieth-century giants in conservation, Aldo Leopold and Wendell Berry. I do this because they are important, because conservation needs acknowledged leaders, and because both have so powerfully borne witness to the essential task of fostering change. Leopold and Berry, of course, are hardly the only writers who deserve study. But if we do not know these two—and in their subtle complexity, few of us probably do—then they provide logical places to start. They are invaluable polestars for anyone who would take conservation seriously.

If I am right in asserting that conservationists are too busy or otherwise disinclined to think seriously about core ideas, I invite the reader's challenge: Why write a book on a topic that few people are likely to read? Serious conservation volumes rarely draw sizeable audiences. This one will likely fare little better, deliberately small though it is. But audiences are as important for their quality as well their size. A few thousand readers—indeed, even a few hundred, seriously engaged—are enough to change the tenor of the cause, to infuse it with new ways to think and talk.

As for the usual excuses—that working conservationists are already too busy, that their rhetoric needs to reach ordinary people where they are—they are true enough but not persuasive. Not every conservationist needs to study thoroughly the underpinnings of the movement. But some do. And those who do then need to help others understand conservation's ecological, historical, moral, and philosophical foundations. The truth is, conservation is a highly complex undertaking. Pieces of it are easily grasped, but the whole of it emphatically is not. We should be led by amateurs—those who labor out of love. But love is no substitute for probing thought and well-crafted strategies. As for the rhetoric, it does need to remain simple and sensible. But a variety of messages meet that test, some better aimed than others. It's the aiming that has been the problem.

Ideas have consequences. To secure good consequences, we need good ideas. To produce good ideas, we need to lean harder at the wheel.

CHAPTER 1

The Four Faces
of Resistance

I n one of several essays lamenting the decline of
his home countryside and farm communities
like it, Kentucky writer-farmer Wendell Berry
comments pointedly on what he perceives as
the fading away of old political distinctions. Long-
standing political dichotomies, Berry tells us, have
become confusingly meaningless. Communists and
capitalists, Democrats and Republicans, liberals and
conservatives: all have bowed down to supranational

corporations and to the juggernaut of the global economy. None takes interest in food quality, land health, or the plight of struggling communities, urban and rural. All show contempt for country life and country places. For a person concerned about land and land-based cultures, old political camps are hard to tell apart.[1]

Although he is hardly a man filled with hope, Berry sees signs that a more honest political order is emerging. On one side is a political party that views local communities as valueless and hence dispensable: the party of the global economy, as Berry terms it, the party now plainly in charge. Opposing this party is one that seeks to preserve land and culture, viewing neighborhoods and local communities as "the proper place and frame of reference for responsible work."[2] This is the party of the local community, and it is only now becoming aware of itself, Berry argues. Though it remains weak and widely scattered, its resources are real and its potential is vast.

Berry's observations are good ones for conservationists to weigh as they take stock of where they are and what lies ahead. The world is indeed a place of conflict, one where powerful resistance awaits those who endeavor to save, restore, connect, and heal. What Berry describes as clashing parties others might characterize in less institutional terms: as opposing ideologies, perhaps, or as alternative value schemes. But the conflict, however phrased, is as real as it is grave: those who would stoke the market inferno with anything that burns stand face-to-face with those who are alarmed by the mounting costs of doing so.

Useful as Berry's dichotomy is, however, one wonders whether it cuts to the true root of current conflicts over lands and communities. People may willingly serve the global economy, but how many of them really applaud it as an intrinsic good? How many campaigns are openly fought under its transnational banner? If the global economy were the only foe, conservationists ought to have more to show for their work. Without powerful allies, that is, Berry's party of the global economy should not be enjoying anything like its current success.

If the conservation movement is going to chart a successful path in coming decades, it needs to know clearly what it is up against. Berry is right, no doubt, in putting the community and its fate at the center of things. But the force pressing against communities is not the global economy so much as it is the ideology that undergirds it—the ideology of ardent individualism, the constellation of values that exalts people as individuals and seeks to liberate them from restraint. Sound communities can exist at all levels, from local to global. Indeed, communities need to exist at levels well above the local to confront problems that require action on a larger scale. What corrodes such communities is not global thought per se but rather the ethos of the self-centered individual, the person who insists on the right to grab and consume with little regard for neighbors, future generations, and other forms of life.

A sound conservation ethic is, fundamentally, an ethic of community, based on interconnection and interdependence. What pushes against such an ethic is not a single opponent but rather a suite of cultural opponents. And they are all the more influential because of the friendly faces they commonly present. Each of them has a good side, for each has helped the American nation to flourish. Yet, like all good things, these cultural elements are good only in moderation; they are good when kept in their proper places.

Environmental degradation is a symptom of a flawed culture, as historians such as Donald Worster have told us in some detail.[3] To halt that degradation, conservationists need to confront these underlying cultural flaws. In the case of the United States, ironically, they largely take the form of excesses of virtue. They take the form, that is, of cultural beliefs and practices that honor the individual human and individual rights but do so in ways that threaten the well-being of the collective whole.

In recent decades, the conservation movement seems to have lost sight of its necessary role as cultural critic. Too often it forgets that it is, at root, a champion of the community as such, a defender of nature's interconnected entirety. For the movement to make further progress, it needs to regain its communitarian grounding.

Perhaps the best way to appreciate where conservation now stands is to back up and reconsider the mature thought of the leading conservationist of the past century, Aldo Leopold. Leopold has hardly been conservation's only major intellect, but he remains the dominant one, long after his death in 1948. To identify the main elements of his thought, especially the messages he thought the public most needed to hear, is to gain a useful vantage point for assessing the current situation.

As a lover of the entire land community, Leopold belonged to a minority strand of American culture. As he so famously put it in his *Sand County Almanac,* he was one of those who preferred to live with and among things "natural, wild, and free," one who viewed "the chance to find a pasque-flower" as inalienable a right as free speech.[4]

Leopold is remembered chiefly for his land ethic, summed up in his essay of that name: "A thing is right when it tends to preserve the integrity, stability, and beauty of the biotic community. It is wrong when it tends otherwise."[5] So familiar are these sentences that it is easy to overlook the complexity of them and to forget that the land ethic was merely one part, albeit a central one, of Leopold's finely argued, wide-ranging critique of the modern age.[6]

From the ample written legacy Leopold left behind, it is possible to tease out four elements of his thought that are especially useful for conservationists charting the path ahead. As the four elements make clear, conservation for Leopold focused on the totality of nature as an interconnected whole and on the need to counteract the chief forces—market economics and private property above all—that fueled harmful land-use choices.

The land community. Early in his professional career as a forester and wildlife manager, Leopold gained a strong sense of the interconnection of all life. His experiences in the Southwest, where overgrazing caused harms that rippled throughout the landscape, led him to see how managers needed to address land as an integrated system, not as a collection of discrete resources.[7] Reading in philosophy led him down a similar path, toward a sense of the organismic characteristics of natural systems. Soon Leopold's expanding ecological wisdom provided an empirical and theoretical base for this intuitive sentiment.[8] The land was a community, he sensed. Its parts were interrelated in ways that reminded him of complex machines. They were interrelated, too, in ways similar to the organs of a body and the cells within an organ. These analogies were not exact, Leopold knew, just as it was not precisely right to equate the biota and a human community. But metaphors were useful tools in bringing home the basic truths of interconnection and interdependence.

During the final decade of his life this land-as-community idea stood at the center of Leopold's thought. He routinely began with it when he spoke about conservation to general audiences. "We abuse land because we regard it as a commodity belonging to us," Leopold asserted in his *Almanac*. "When we see land as a community to which we belong, we may begin to use it with love and respect."[9] An ecological understanding of land was essential if conservation was to succeed. Rural landowners especially needed to embrace this perspective. Only with it could they act with the sensitivity required to use land well.

Land health. One of Leopold's chief complaints was the fragmentation that characterized the conservation movement of his day. The conservation workers were many, but they often pushed in different directions. Conservation was a "house divided," Leopold protested; it lacked a philosophy and would not get far without one.[10] The result, too often, was that conservationists worked at cross-purposes—some promoting productive forests, others soil conservation, others the efficient use of waterways, still others the protection of wildlife habitat—in the process employing tools that could and did clash. Leopold illustrated the danger: "I cite in evidence the C.C.C. [Civilian Conservation Corps] crew which chopped down one of the few remaining eagle's nests in northern Wisconsin, in the name of 'timber stand improvement.' To be sure, the tree was dead, and according to the rules, constituted a fire risk."[11] Conflict in the field had secondary effects as well, for so long as conservationists promoted competing agendas, public action could stall.[12]

Leopold's worries about conflicts within conservation soon merged with his ideas about land as community. To coordinate efforts, conservation needed an overall goal, a common target at which all conservationists could aim. Given that land worked as an integrated system, the logical aim was one linked to the ability of the system as such to function over time. For Leopold, there was "only one soil, one flora, one fauna, and one people," which was to say "only one conservation problem."[13] A single problem called for a single resolution, however diverse the means to achieve it.

In an important essay in 1935 Leopold explored the principal signs of a land community beset with disease.[14] Soon he would assemble those signs into affirmative if vague statements about what it meant for land to possess health. The land was a community, Leopold realized, and communities could be more or less healthy. Conservation was properly aimed at promoting that health. Land health, then, was the much-needed conservation goal.[15]

"Land health," Leopold wrote in 1944, "is the capacity for self-renewal in the soils, waters, plants, and animals that collectively comprise the land."[16] "Health expresses the cooperation of the interdependent parts: soil, water, plants, animals, and people," he had written two years earlier. "It implies collective self-renewal and collective self-maintenance."[17] Central to Leopold's understanding of land health was the ability of land to retain its font of fertility—its soil. Fertility was preserved only when sufficient types and numbers of species were present to keep basic nutrients cycling through the system efficiently. Land is healthy "when its food chains are so organized as to be able to circulate the same food an indefinite number of times."[18] Only under such circumstances would the soil—"the repository of food between its successive trips through the chains"—retain its fertility and produce abundant, nutritious yields.[19]

In August of 1946, Leopold was asked by leaders of a new political party to draft its platform on conservation. In his brief response, Leopold made no mention of the specific challenges about which he knew so much—wildlife, forestry, wilderness, soil conservation. Instead, he pointed toward the polestar: "[T]he health of the land as a whole, rather than the supply of its constituent 'resources,' is what needs conserving. Land, like other things, has the capacity for self-renewal (i.e. for permanent productivity) only when its natural parts are present, and functional. It is a dangerous fallacy to assume that we are free to discard or change any part of the land we do not find 'useful' (such as flood plains, marshes, and wild floras and faunas). Too violent modification of the natural order has repeatedly disorganized the land's capacity for self-renewal."[20]

Leopold described healthy land as "stable," not to suggest that natural systems were static but in the more specific sense of land that retained its ability to cycle nutrients effectively and thus maintain its soil fertility.[21] In order to do that, the land needed to have integrity, by which Leopold meant the biotic parts necessary for this nutrient cycling to take place.[22] Leopold used "stability" and "integrity" in tandem as a shorthand expression for land health, most famously when summing up his land ethic, his ardent call to promote the land's stability (its ability to cycle nutrients), its integrity (the diversity of parts needed to sustain stability), and its beauty.[23] It was the land ethic that transformed the goal of overall health into an individual but shared duty: "A land ethic, then, reflects the existence of an ecological conscience, and this in turn reflects a conviction of individual responsibility for the health of the land."[24]

Conservation economics. A third element of Leopold's conservation thought regarded the economic realities of conserving land, particularly private land.[25] How private owners used their land materially affected the surrounding land community. Because of that, and because communities endured far beyond any single owner's life span, the public had a weighty interest in how a landowner behaved.

As Leopold assessed the economics of sound land use, he was quick to see that conservation paid dividends, yet the dividends were largely ones that landowners acting alone could not capture. The benefits spread to the entire community, of which the landowner was only a small part. When all landowners conserved, each of them might gain. But conservation by an isolated owner rarely made financial sense.

For Leopold, these economic realities posed a challenge worthy of careful research. Repeatedly he would propose it as a topic: "the formulation of mechanisms for protecting the public interest in private land."[26] Existing institutions simply did not attend to the matter: "The present legal and economic structure, having been evolved on a more resistant terrain (Europe) and before the machine age, contains no suitable ready-made mechanisms for protecting the public interest in private land. It evolved at a time when the public had no interest in land except to help tame it."[27]

Leopold devoted himself to the challenge of advancing conservation interests in the face of conflicting financial benefits, identifying the tools available and assessing the merits of each. Economic incentives, education, legal restraints, boycotts, social ostracism, community-based conservation measures—Leopold considered them all, only to conclude that none would do the trick. "How can private landowners be induced to use their land conservatively?" Leopold repeatedly asked himself. "This question heretofore determined only the choice of method for executing a conservation program (for example, the choice between education, subsidy, compulsion, or public ownership). Now, it seems to me, it takes rank with technological unemployment as one of the critical tests of 'The American Way.'"[28]

Images of ownership. For Leopold, the leading conservation challenge of his day was starkly posed by the individual landowner living on and using a single tract of land. For the land to become healthy, this owner had to act well. Achieving good land use was difficult because economic factors were so unfavorable. Added to the dismal economics was the whole matter of what it meant to own land, legally and culturally. So long as ownership gave a person the right to ignore the common good, true conservation was doomed.

Leopold was no legal scholar and knew little about private property's history as an institution. Had he known more, particularly about the many forms private ownership has taken in different times and places, he might have called even louder for institutional change. Yet his instincts were sound and he was prepared to act on them. Private ownership as commonly understood was itself a conservation problem, Leopold decided. Ownership gave landowners too much freedom to degrade the landscape to further personal interests. Ownership was a matter of individual rights, and hardly at all about limits and duties.

Early in his career Leopold raised the possibility that laws one day might force owners to take better care of their lands. In a provocative passage penned in the 1920s, he speculated that landownership in time would "carry with it the obligation to so use and protect it with respect to erosion that it is not a menace to other landowners and the public." One day it would become illegal, he predicted, for landowners to allow erosion "to menace the public streams, reservoirs, irrigation projects," and neighboring lands. Such "enforced responsibility of landowners," though, was "of the future."[29] Until then and to help the change come about, conservationists should push hard for cultural change.

These four points do little more than identify the main strands of Leopold's thought, leaving untouched its richness and subtlety. Nonetheless, they suffice to ground a lesson about needed change that conservationists might usefully keep fresh.

For Leopold, conservation posed a serious challenge to the practices and understandings of his day, and it would succeed only if it brought about major cultural change. Minor adjustments were simply not enough. To accomplish significant change, conservation required a solid grounding in ecology and economics; when "devoid of critical understanding either of the land, or of economic land use," conservation could be "futile, or even dangerous."[30] Conservation also required "an internal change in our intellectual emphases, loyalties, affections, and convictions."[31] People needed to "change their ideas about what land is for"; and "[t]o change ideas about what land is for is to change ideas about what anything is for."[32]

If Aldo Leopold was the leading conservation intellect of the first half of the twentieth century, his successor in matters relating to private land use has undoubtedly been Wendell Berry, who from his farm along the Kentucky River has written for decades on the ways that people inhabit their homes.

In his many writings Berry has added useful pieces to the conservation legacy amassed by Leopold. He has brought more of the social community into the land-use picture and linked that community, more strongly than Leopold had, to past and future generations. He has expanded Leopold's critique of land-use economics while adding force and clarity to Leopold's call for a new vision of private landownership. And, like Leopold, Berry has put the community and its long-term health at the top of his conservation agenda. Yet Berry has met similar frustration in his attempts to defend that community against hostile forces. After decades of work, he, too, would fall back on the need for people to better themselves, one by one, by embracing a sounder land ethic and by taking seriously the age-old call to love one another.[33]

Wendell Berry grew up in the 1930s and 1940s with a connection to the land rare for Americans at any time.[34] He was born in the rural neighborhood where his parents and all of his grandparents had been born and where his great-grandparents had lived. Drawn to his grandfather's farm at an early age, Berry learned to work fields with draft horses and to manage a diverse family homestead.[35] Early in the 1960s Berry's writing career took him away from his northern Kentucky homeland; his experiences included a year studying in California, travels in Europe, and a stint teaching at New York University. Only then, having seen the urban world close up, was he ready to head back home. Even working in Manhattan, though, Berry remained mindful of nature and of the grip it had on his soul, mindful that nature's forces were ever restless, struggling to rise up whenever humans relaxed their firm hold:

> In the empty lot—a place
> not natural, but wild—among
> the trash of human absence,
>
> the slough and shamble,
> of the city's seasons, a few
> old locusts bloom.[36]

By the mid-1960s, his mind and heart darkened by the deepening Asian war, Berry quit the city and returned to his native soil. His journey was not to a clean, healthy land—to the Arcadian place where protagonists of pastoral tales have typically started life anew—but to a landscape that humans had long scarred and misused, including the particular marginal acres that Berry and his family chose to make their own. The countryside of his upbringing needed good human stewards, better ones than it had had. He was eager to become one of them.

Writing soon after his return, Berry remembered vividly a day in the spring of 1945 when he was ten and the world war was winding down. With a companion he borrowed a small boat during high flood and journeyed foolishly into the fast-flowing Kentucky River. The adventure was a grand one, or so it seemed once the two were home safe and the scolding from their worried elders had subsided. The Kentucky River had its seasons, angry and powerful ones, yet the particular flood that imperiled young Berry was not nature's doing alone. Neither was the flood a few years earlier, the one back in 1937 that lifted riverside cabins off their foundations. "These were modern floods," Berry realized, "and man-made. Too many of the mountain slopes along the headwater streams had been denuded by thoughtless lumbering and thoughtless farming. Too little humus remained in the soil to hold the rains. After this second flood more of the old houses built near the river in earlier times would be abandoned."[37]

Mindful of this troubled history and painfully aware of the economic forces pushing his homeland down, Berry determined nonetheless to take up the reins dropped by earlier landowners. He would labor as best he could, working with nature and respecting its limits. He would protect his soil by planting clover and slowly rebuilding its dark fund of life. Guiding this work, he later explained, was an overriding desire: "to make myself responsibly at home both in this world and in my native and chosen place." His was "a long term desire," as he described, "proposing the work not of a lifetime but of generations."[38]

Berry's observations about land and land use were colored by his years spent conversing with respected farmers and wooing the soil. Experience and intuition forged in him a strong sense of land as a community, just as Aldo Leopold had declared. They also fostered a sense that land use was good only when it sustained the health of that community, human members included. Land health was "the one value," the one "absolute good" that upheld the entire web of life.[39] When speaking on the subject, Berry has frequently borrowed a line from English reformer Sir Albert Howard, who urged readers to understand "the whole problem of health in soil, plant, and animal, and man as one great subject."[40] For Berry, the community as such is the smallest unit that might properly be called healthy. "To speak of the health of an isolated individual," given the individual's dependence on the whole, "is a contradiction in terms."[41]

Even more than Leopold, Wendell Berry has regularly spoken about land use as an ethical issue—indeed, a religious one. To abuse land is immoral as well as unwise, and this truth needs to be told. At the same time, Berry understands the complexity of good land use and how difficult it is for anyone to use a tract well. Mistakes are easily made. Lessons can come at high cost. Leopold portrayed the individual landowner as a member of the land community. Berry goes further, linking that owner to the surrounding social order and explaining how one owner's success can depend upon the existence of a shared body of local land-use wisdom. In settled agrarian cultures, practical ways of using land are learned slowly and handed down from generation to generation.[42]

Because good land use takes time to emerge out of frontier conditions, the well-being of land is necessarily linked to the viability of the resident social order. Good landowners plan for the next generation, confident that it will carry on their labors. Conservative land use is most typical of owners who equate ownership with stewardship and who sense an accountability to those who come next. Yet communities that foster this ethic can endure only when the economics of communal life are favorable. Community economics, in turn, depend on the economics, good or bad, of operating the individual farm.

Even more than Leopold, Berry has addressed the challenge of farm economics, particularly the market forces that have ruthlessly depressed small towns. So competitive is farming that few owners earn more than modest incomes, especially on marginal lands. Free trade is an important element of this problem, particularly global trade, which forces owners to slash costs and to operate on ever-bigger scales. Bigger scales, though, mean fewer farmers, which means fewer people to patronize community stores and fewer children in local schools. These losses, in turn, mean closed stores and schools, declining towns, and a landscape bled of people.[43]

In his extensive writing, Berry has added usefully to our understanding of land conservation. He has spoken eloquently about the ways that one landowner's success is linked to the well-being of the surrounding community. He has probed the powerful economic forces that undercut shared life and make good land use so difficult. Even when community members are all devoted stewards—a rare happenstance—local communities are buffeted by outside forces. In practice they struggle, and largely fail, in their attempts to hold on.

Both as writer and as member of his native community, Berry has labored to find ways for local economies to endure.[44] Some farmers have turned to specialty markets for high-valued produce. Others grow food for community-supported agriculture projects and farmers' markets. Timber-based communities have sought out value-added local industries, so that forest products shipped from an area can yield greater returns. Even in combination, however, these measures and others like them have had only modest effects. Prospects remain bleak.

In the end, Berry the reformer has found himself stalled, much as Leopold did. Economic and social forces push hard against landowners, and they respond as agribusiness companies and university scientists tell them to respond: by embracing practices that slowly sap their lands and economies. Communities need better ways to fight back. The tools that Berry has identified, however, like the tools of Leopold, are simply not up to the task. Berry criticizes distant governments for failing to protect communities against outside forces, but how can this be done consistently with America's cultural traditions?[45]

Like Leopold, Wendell Berry has concluded that real progress must await social growth. Friends of the land can only hope and pray for a new ethical order in which people value natural systems, in which they warmly embrace the work, social relations, and inner peacefulness that are necessary pillars of settled communal life.[46] One cannot be optimistic, and Berry is not.[47] But where else can hope find refuge?

When Aldo Leopold began his professional career, conservation was mostly a matter of protecting discrete resource flows, particularly wildlife, timber, and clean water, along with the human economies dependent on them. Wild areas, preserved for their recreational and spiritual benefits, were valued as distinct enclaves more than as vital parts of larger landscapes. By the time he died in 1948, Leopold had considerably enriched this base, intellectually, ethically, and aesthetically. He had bridged the conservation-preservation split in ways that rendered it artificial. He had successfully mixed utility and beauty, ethics and aesthetics.[48]

Leopold understood, as many others then did not and still do not, that to promote conservation is to stand up for community and to fight against fragmentation. The key battleground was the privately owned land parcel. It was there that conservation would stand or fall. Private land was declining because of bad decisions by landowners. Landowners, in turn, acted as they did because of unfavorable land-use economics, poor ecological understandings, and immature ethical and aesthetic ideals. Real change would need to address these deficiencies.

Wendell Berry usefully built on Leopold's work by embedding his predecessor's ill-behaving landowner into a social community and a local economy. As he did so, Berry shifted part of the blame for poor land use up to the communal level. Without healthy communities, Berry explained, even well-meaning owners could often do little. Bad land use had structural causes; until they were solved conservation would remain cosmetic. Yet having clarified the challenges, Berry was unsure how to respond to them, particularly to the domineering global economy. Farm towns had become pawns of outside forces, and he could see little to do about it.

Leopold and Berry, of course, have not been the only conservation voices of the past century. Others have stood with them. Few writers, however, have been as conspicuous in standing up for communities and embracing the advice that Leopold offered to all conservationists: "throw your weight around on matters of right and wrong in land use."[49] Few writers have seen so starkly that conservationists have a nasty cultural fight on their hands.

Conservationists taking stock of things today might usefully draw upon this conservation wisdom. The dominant social force at work today is indeed the market. With every decade, it wields greater influence on the ways we see nature and use our lands. To build on Berry's work, then, as Berry has built on Leopold's, it is essential for us to understand this pervasive institution.

Markets operate on the principle of competition. Free trade widens that competition, imposing ever-stronger pressures on market participants to cut their costs (in the case of working lands by eroding soil, deranging water flows, bulldozing wildlife habitat, proliferating exotics, and replacing complex biotic communities with monocultures). Markets also work by means of fragmentation, by treating people as individual consumers and producers and by dividing nature into its parts—some of them assigned market values, most afforded none. In the worldview of the market, neighborhoods, communities, and ecological systems have no direct value since none are for sale.

In a world shaped by the capitalist market, almost everything is up for grabs. Natural systems count for nothing unless market participants voluntarily choose to honor them. As for the future, individuals are nominally free to weigh it as they like. But competition imposes a stern discipline: those who act with restraint can easily lose out to those who ignore the future. Then there are the problems that come from the high specialization that the market requires. Low-cost production is commonly achievable only by those who fill a specific market niche. If the system itself is destructive, of lands or of people, there's little the specialist can do except participate or drop out.

Many forms of land destruction arise as detrimental "externalities"—that is, as harms that one market participant generates and freely imposes on neighbors.[50] The more fragmented a landscape is and the stronger the many competitive pressures, the greater this problem can be.[51] Although Aldo Leopold never used the term *externalities,* the idea forcefully influenced his thoughts on private land. To divide an integrated landscape into private shares was to skew the economics of good land use. Along with the problem of externalities were the many factors that led landowners to act unwisely even within the boundaries of their tracts, the all-too-common cognitive, ethical, and economic shortcomings that Leopold confronted so directly in his writings.

As a mechanism for resource allocation, the market's weaknesses and biases are profound. The market deals with people as individual consumers and producers, not as communal members. Government processes of study and taking action, weak though they often are, are replaced in the market by the manipulations of advertisers and the sound bites of industry. A further problem here: the market is efficient only in supplying people with goods and services that they can enjoy individually, with little or no sharing. Most conservation goods (migratory birds and healthy rivers, for instance) are not of this type, particularly ecological and landscape goals. (They are public goods, to use the economic term.) Mythology notwithstanding, the market can do a lousy job giving us what we really want.[52]

These days, the market has vocal, influential advocates, legions of them, who praise it lavishly as a method of ordering affairs and who applaud it for great accomplishments, all the while downplaying or ignoring its limitations. Their enthusiasm, so starkly uncritical at times, is at once an obstacle on the path and a revealing sign of where we stand as a people.

For communities to be healthy, their defenders need to craft effective ways to contain these powerful forces. The market needs firm boundaries if it is to respect lands and people. Private property must become less of a shield. Particularly as technology advances and populations rise, citizen governance, aimed at protecting the community and its health, becomes all the more vital.[53]

One wonders, given the plentiful evidence of degradation, why conservationists face such resistance today. Why is it so hard to contend with the forces of fragmentation? The term *community* conjures up good images for most Americans. Public opinion polls show overwhelming support for environmental protection.[54] Save for free market fanatics, no one stands up to defend self-centered behavior. Given this broad support for conservation, and given that markets as such—and advertisers and big industry in particular—enjoy at best mixed public favor, why has conservation so often stalled?

The answers are not hard to find, for they appear in the news media and in public speech nearly every day. Organized conservation, it is said, conflicts with core values of American culture, particularly when conservation means binding rules and regulations. To put it otherwise: blocking acceptance of conservation are not so much the familiar faces of the market—development, individualism, and selfishness—but far friendlier faces, the cultural emblems that make America what it is. Conservation's opponents have appropriated these emblems after defining them in ways that make conservation duties appear costly, even un-American. It is familiar strategy in the culture wars, using cultural emblems as weapons. To the conservation side, the damage has been great.

Liberty. Foremost on the cultural list is the powerful ideal of individual liberty, the bedrock of American culture. Liberty is the ability of a person in isolation to develop and implement a vision of the good life. Liberty means freedom from restraint as one goes about daily life.

The difficulty with this ideal is that it contains no brake on its power. Liberty resists all restraint, however reasonable and necessary. Also absent from it is a principled way to determine when the liberty of one person should yield to the liberty of another. Particularly in land-use settings, where actions on one parcel can spread wide ecologically, one owner's actions can materially disrupt the lives of many others. Where does one person's liberty end and another's begin? Then there is the critical matter of individuals who want to exercise their *positive* liberty by joining with neighbors to engage in communal lawmaking, as by imposing rules to protect land health. How does the value of this positive liberty compare to the negative liberty of the individual who wants to act without restraint?[55]

Democracy. Related to liberty and similarly deployed against conservation is the familiar face of democracy, the power of ordinary people to govern their lives, free of kings, oligarchies, and other higher powers. In a democracy, sovereignty is exercised by the *demos*—the people—rather than by a monarch or ruling class.[56] But how do people exercise this power? Majority rule, one way of exercising popular power, regularly produces laws that many people oppose. From the perspective of conservation's opponents, majority-run government can appear as an alien, intrusive power, interfering with private lives and controlled by special interests.

Like liberty, democracy as popularly understood is simply incoherent intellectually. It leaves unresolved the critical question of majority rule versus individual choice. Incoherence, in turn, opens the way for image manipulation. Libertarians ask: Isn't the market the most democratic of all institutions? Isn't the market the arena in which people can form their choices individually and act upon them with little restraint? Don't land-use laws conflict with true democratic rule?

Private property. Just as revered as the political ideals of liberty and democracy is the institution of private property, which has risen high in the pantheon of cultural icons since the fall of the Soviet Union.[57] Though the differences between the United States and the Soviet Union were countless—most conspicuously in the responsiveness of government to the popular will—many Americans have pointed to private property as the key distinction: the Soviet Union fell because it lacked private property, the United States has thrived because it respects private rights.[58] The explanation sounds convincing, even though grossly incomplete. One reason the story has caught on is that it taps into the unquestioned power of secure private property to foster economic enterprise. Private property does bring good things, and the success of the United States is certainly linked to it.

Yet private property, like liberty and democracy, loses its clarity as soon as one approaches it. Again, the land-use context offers good evidence. The landowner who drains wet areas can cause flooding affecting the landowner downstream. In such a circumstance, how can the law protect private rights? Is property respected by allowing the upstream owner to drain or by protecting the downstream owner against flooding? In facile discussions of private property, the downstream owner is typically overlooked. The simple, much-used paradigm conflict is one that pits the individual owner against the state, with no mention of neighboring landowners or other community members.[59]

Private property shares ambiguities with liberty and democracy, to which it is closely linked. Considered abstractly, private ownership includes no means of deciding where one person's property rights end and another's begin when neighboring land uses clash. It includes no way to decide when the property rights of one landowner should be limited by the legitimate desires of other property-owning community members to enjoy a healthy, beautiful landscape.[60]

Equality. Finally, there is the friendly cultural ideal of equality, which stands alongside the other three, even though strong tensions exist among them. Equality is the most incomplete of the four cultural ideals in that it operates only when linked to independent understandings of fairness and human rights.[61] The truth is, no two people are identical. Given the inevitable differences, the question then becomes: When do we ignore the differences between two people, thus treating them as equal, and when in the name of equality do we take the differences into account? When it comes to voting, gender and race are irrelevant but age and citizenship are not. Again and again, equality raises the issue of which differences we consider and which we ignore. In isolation, equality never supplies an answer. It is the bluntest of tools.

Equality is particularly troublesome in the context of land-use disputes when it is linked to private property. Is equality fostered by a law that treats landowner A and landowner B the same when each wants to build homes or graze cows or cut trees? Is it violated when a law allows A to proceed with development but stops B from doing the same? To answer such questions we need to distinguish sharply between a law that views A and B differently as *people* and a law that treats A's *land* differently from B's land. To distinguish between A and B as people might well be improper. But land-use laws rarely do that. They deal instead with land, and two land parcels are never truly the same. If A's land is submerged and B's land is high and dry, a law might wisely distinguish between the two without violating any well-conceived ideal of equality. In public discourse, though, we typically pay attention to the owners as people. And so the cry of unfairness is raised.

We only need listen to the rhetoric of forces resisting land-use rules to see how these four cultural symbols are deployed. Used in combination they ably protect developers, home builders, mining companies, and agribusiness groups. Land-use laws restrict individual liberties, so it is claimed. When imposed by distant governments, and particularly when fueled by the lobbying efforts of interest groups, such laws distort legitimate democratic processes. In all cases, restrictions diminish private property rights, unfairly forcing owners to use their lands to benefit other people, without compensation. Laws that burden some landowners and not others—as nearly all do—also raise the specter of unequal treatment. All in all, land-use laws, it is argued, collide with our cherished ideals.

It is to this constellation of ideas that conservation needs to respond, thoughtfully and forcefully.

To dwell upon the disheartening status of conservation today is to wonder whether the current predicament is not to a large degree self-induced. In their endless flurry of deals, lobbying, and litigation, have conservationists failed to attend to the intellectual and cultural sides of the issue? Have we driven ahead, confident of our bearings, only to find ourselves ambushed in a culture war we are ill prepared to fight?[62]

Opponents of conservation talk openly about this quartet of cultural and political ideals, which are, for them, very much on the public table. Where, though, is the conservation response? What does it mean, to conservationists, to own land privately? As industrial interests see matters, environmental rules interfere with core civil liberties. What do conservationists have to say in rebuttal?

Too often they have nothing to respond, at least not directly. Too often they ignore the issue, or accede implicitly to the accuracy of what opponents contend, arguing only that environmental benefits make the costs worthwhile. More and more, conservationists reject the idea that there even is such a thing as a "conservation perspective" on such issues, priding themselves instead on a plurality of views. But to celebrate plurality in itself is to have no sensible response to opposing claims. In a sound-bite world, in a world of two-sided journalistic stories, a movement that lacks coherence becomes especially easy prey.

More than conservationists realize, the battle over land is being waged as much in the realm of public rhetoric as on the land. And as in most rhetorical battles, the tools of choice are the ideals that Americans have long used to frame their disputes. Because of the pluralism that characterizes conservation, it is hard to generalize about where conservation thought now stands, save to point out, as we must do, that conservation does not present a coherent message to average citizens. The rhetorical deficiencies are many, particularly when we put today's rhetoric side by side with the core ideas of Leopold and Berry.

First, while conservationists feel comfortable talking about emotional attachments to land, they have largely discarded Leopold's language of ecological connection and ecosystem processes. Few talk about land as community, the centerpiece of Leopold's thought. Exceptions do exist, important ones. But to the average listener conservation deals with particular parcels of land that need protecting against human overuse. People are not part of the land community as they were in Leopold's thought; they are only the force that brings about degradation.

The dangers of single-parcel conservation are particularly acute when the parcels being preserved have no people living on them. An oft-repeated criticism is that conservationists care about wild things, not about people. The charge is easily disproved, yet it rarely is. It would lose force if conservationists employed a different rhetoric, if they talked regularly about the health of entire landscapes, people included.

A second rhetorical deficiency is that conservationists (with important exceptions) tend to ignore lands used to meet basic human needs, or if they address them they implicitly portray users as inherently bad. Leopold focused his mature work almost entirely on working lands; Wendell Berry, from his farm, has paid little attention to anything else. As Leopold put it, the conservation challenge is "co-extensive with the map of the United States."[63] The message deserves more prominence than it gets.

A third deficiency of conservation rhetoric is that it rarely engages with the economic assessments of opponents, except to weigh in from to time on cost-benefit analyses. Indeed, the whole field of economics has largely been abandoned to universities and to staffs of libertarian/free market advocacy groups, whose position papers flow forth without end.[64] Conservation is nowhere near as costly as the public assumes. Indeed, one would hardly realize, given the assumptions so commonly accepted, that environmental laws generate economic benefits that exceed their costs, usually by a wide margin.[65] To listen to public officials, mimicking the rhetoric of opposing groups, environmental protection is a luxury when the economy is weak. Conservationists need to dispute this point far better than they have.

Just as disturbing as the inattention to economics is the near silence from conservationists on private property and what it means to own land. There is no need to guess what libertarians think on the subject, for they trumpet their views. Conservation groups, with few exceptions, keep their thoughts to themselves. Leopold, again, is feted but not followed.

This lack of discussion about private property is linked to the reluctance of many conservationists to talk about their work in moral terms, except on the issue of endangered species. Moral language, of course, requires careful use. But moral criticism can address ideas and practices rather than people. It can accentuate the moral good of healthy lands and intact communities without resorting to accusation. Opponents of conservation hardly hesitate to frame liberties and property rights as moral claims. For conservationists to avoid the terminology is to concede the high ground.

Finally, there is the plain fact that, outside the academy, conservation thought has mainly dispensed with all talk of an overall goal. On few issues was the mature Leopold more adamant. Land health for Leopold was the antidote to many ills. It helped coordinate efforts. It helped instill an ecological perspective. Slogans such as "jobs-versus-owls" would persuade far fewer listeners if the conservation cause communicated a well-conceived goal.

In the common understanding, environmentalism is a liberal cause. Classically defined, *liberalism* is a political and cultural perspective that honors the individual human and seeks to free him or her from unfair restraint.[66] Its original opponent was the feudal system, which situated people within layered social orders and enmeshed them in status rules. So powerful has liberalism become, in both its welfare and libertarian forms, that it significantly defines American culture.[67]

Were Leopold alive today, he would know how to talk about the claim (the condemnation, as many see it) that conservation is inherently liberal in the classic sense.[68] As Leopold perceived things, humans inevitably were members of biotic communities. They did not and could not thrive in isolation. Though they were free to throw off all shackles and pursue self-selected goals, they would assuredly harm the land in doing so. Leopold exalted individuals in that he respected their free will and believed that they could lead honorable, ethical lives; the individual did count, and it was to the individual that Leopold addressed his now-famous ethic. At the same time, Leopold openly condemned versions of individualism that dignified narrow pursuits of self-interest; "bogus individualism," he would term it.[69] Ecologically and ethically, humans were integrated into larger systems, whether they knew it or not. Conservation was about mending the communal fabric, not enhancing individual freedoms.

Writing in the same vein, Wendell Berry also honors the individual, but only when the individual stands tall as a responsible community member. In Berry's view, contemporary people need to be tethered to past and future generations if they are to tend the land well.[70] Health comes from respecting nature's limits and from building healthy relationships, not by casting them off.

Despite this communitarian heritage, conservation is showing more and more signs of embracing classic liberalism. In the name of pluralism it invites people as individuals to develop their own ideas about land and to embrace moral views of their own choosing. In doing so, it implicitly denies Leopold's and Berry's beliefs in intrinsic moral values. In its resistance to " top-down" thinking and its enthusiasm for community-based processes, it rejects any overriding goal conceived by leading intellectuals. For conservation to embrace such relativity, abandoning its ecologically informed morality, would be to turn sharply from its core teachings.

Conservation is losing ground—or at least failing to advance as it might, given public opinion—because it shies away from the culture wars. It says too little about the moral and civic ideals that opponents have invoked. If conservation really conflicted with these ideals, the impasse might make sense. But present conflicts have arisen primarily because libertarian and proindustry groups have reshaped and distorted our ideals. Conservation needs to rise to the challenge.

- Conservation needs to speak openly about the conflict in American culture, pitting those who stand up for the communal whole against those who are content to let people do as they please. American audiences don't shy away from conflict; some seem to relish it. Friendly faces and respectful language can remain. It is the underlying clash that needs clear labels: the Battle for Community, the Struggle for Responsible Living.

- Conservation also needs better ways to display the tragic consequences of fragmenting lands and people—legally, economically, and socially. Conservation must be—and be seen as—a powerful antidote to this fragmentation.

- Even more urgent is the need for the cause to develop a thoughtful critique of the capitalist market.[71] So infatuated has America become with the market that it understands poorly what the institution can and cannot do. In equal need of scrutiny is the claim that environmental laws reduce the productivity of the market. Some do, but many have just the opposite effect: they remedy market failings and thus aid overall efficiency. On economic issues as on moral ones, conservationists need to do their homework and then charge ahead.

- Related to the market issue is the institution of private property, and here, too, conservationists can do better. The vision of private ownership put forward by conservation opponents is seriously miscast.[72] It rests on bad law, bad history, and bad policy. Conservation is not about rejecting private property, which in its place is wonderfully useful. It is about pressing for much-needed reform.

- Similar work needs to be done in crafting messages that address the other ideals cited by conservation's opponents. Liberty has a positive side as well as a negative one; it is freedom *to,* as well as freedom *from.* Liberty's positive side respects the power of people to join with others to make rules for their common good. In like manner, democracy comes in many forms, one of the most venerable being majority rule based on one person, one vote. Strong individual rights, the kind that conservation's opponents so ardently deploy, restrain these democratic processes. On this issue, too, conservationists must not give in.

CHAPTER 2

Five Paths and Their Values

One piece of advice commonly offered to inexperienced short-story writers is to begin a narrative not at the beginning, but close to the end. Start in the thick of things and fill in the background as needed, and the shorter the story the closer to the end one ought to begin. "The Jilting of Granny Weatherall," for instance, a well-wrought tale by Katherine Anne Porter, begins with Mrs. Weatherall on her deathbed. We witness her final hours and through asides learn about her life, the suffering she endured, the choices she made and how they affected her plight. Much of the background, though, goes unsaid or is merely implied, and we are left to read between the lines—just as Ms. Porter wants us to do and enables us to do. We are left to piece together the ethical and perceptual lay of the land.

This story-writing suggestion is usefully recalled when one attempts to survey academic thought about environmental issues, particularly writing that deals with environmental law and other practical embodiments of environmental policy. (In the legal and policy-setting arenas, the term *environmental* has shown few signs of yielding to *conservation* or other terms.) Intentionally, perhaps, but more likely from a hurry to get to where the action is, most environmental policy scholars have heeded this literary advice. Articles typically begin by laying out a problem or issue, but they rarely start at the beginning of things, any more than Ms. Porter does when she opens the scene with Mrs. Weatherall dying. The typical environmental piece is merely the final installment of an argumentative narrative, where the forces finally clash and a resolution is achieved.

In Ms. Porter's story Granny Weatherall is the narrator, but to understand the story we need to recognize quickly that she is not a reliable one. So part of the job of reading is to get inside the narrator's mind, identifying the author's hints and recognizing how the narrator is distorting, editing, and coloring life. Then, too, no story exists apart from its author (despite schools of literary criticism that periodically argue the contrary), and so to grasp a story fully it is helpful to know something about the background voice. We need to know how the author came to the first page of the story as well as how the characters got there. Environmental policy scholarship is not all that different. The typical way of reading policy-related writing is to look forward in time, to see where the author's conclusions might lead. But as much or more can be learned by taking backward glances, determining insofar as possible the author's intellectual and moral path to the opening page.

Scholarship about environmental law and policy comes in more varieties now than it ever has. And much of that variety has to do with the paths authors have taken and the motives and perceptions that drive them to write. Three decades ago, people wrote about environmental concerns for obvious reasons: the problems were unmistakable and needed solving; self-ish businesses and misguided governments were the apparent enemies; and the battle lines were clear. The primary goals were to safeguard human health and to save key wilderness areas, exotic species, and other natural gems. Policies were crafted and then, one by one, incorporated into law.

Today the situation is far different, for reasons that are not apparent on the printed page—indeed, part of the current weakness of environmental scholarship arises because so much of the ideological and intellectual background is left off the page. And the cost of starting in media res is far greater here than in literary realms. In fictional writing, a reader who misses the background cannot enjoy the story fully; he cannot appreciate its many resonances and pursue its suggestive leads. In the scholarly realm, the deficiency is more fundamental. A reader who fails to chart the author's path cannot engage in the indispensable readerly task of critically evaluating the author's work.

Environmental policy scholarship can be loosely characterized by isolating five different scholarly *types,* reflective of the several moral and intellectual paths diverse authors follow to the opening page.[1] The real world is not this clean, of course. Real scholars never adhere to one type all the time, and there are always outlying scholars who defy simple categorization. Still, the basic types have enough integrity to be helpful for the purpose at hand—to identify and clarify distinct intellectual approaches, enabling us to think clearly about them and spot their underlying differences.[2]

The five types are these: *libertarians, simple fixers* (a group with two overlapping subgroups: the *free marketers,* and the *technological fixers*), *dispute resolvers, progressive reformers,* and *land community advocates.* These types are arranged roughly from right to left on the political spectrum, though the last type fits uneasily due to its communitarian leanings.[3]

Three decades ago, *libertarians* did not write much about environmental issues. Their attention was largely focused elsewhere. Government was the problem; it had become too invasive in people's lives and violated individual liberties. Today environmental laws are part of that invasion, a particularly annoying part as many libertarians see it, and they require pruning if not a significant thinning. In the worldview of the libertarian type, the moral landscape is simple. People alone count, morally and practically, and they count as individuals rather than as families or neighborhoods or communities. Maximum liberty is the goal, defined negatively and with reference only to governmental (rather than private) invasions, with minimal government the desired corollary. People achieve their goals acting alone and in voluntary cooperation with others, not through means that coerce dissenters. Environmental problems, with few or no exceptions, are either adequately solved or exaggerated. Any lingering problems are viewed as matters of resource allocation, best addressed by expanding the market's reach and improving its operation. Protecting individual liberty, again negatively defined, is the primary moral imperative and the chief if not sole reason for government's existence. In the case of environmental degradation, governmental coercion is inappropriate except when degradation violates individual property rights.

The second type, the *simple fixers,* indicates scholars who believe or assume that environmental degradation stems chiefly from deficiencies either in the market or in modern technology. Scholars of this type vary in their appraisal of environmental problems. Some think the main problems are largely solved but that the solutions can be improved. For these scholars, today's top job is to rewrite laws and regulations to achieve greater economic and technological efficiency, reducing the size of government in the process. Other simple fixers recognize that some problems are not yet solved—runoff water pollution, for instance—which leads them to propose an expansion or refinement of the market or the stimulation of new technology. Proposed market improvements take various, now-familiar forms: internalizing external harms (and, less often, benefits); reducing transaction costs; defining property rights more completely, clearly, and securely; and facilitating markets in previously untraded entitlements.[4] Technology improvements are stimulated either by creating financial incentives (preferably market-based) for technology developers or, less desirably, by specifying exact environmental goals for particular entities and then giving those entities wide technological latitude to achieve them.

On the middle path are the *dispute resolvers*. Scholars of this type are most true to the legal tradition; they are primarily lawyers, political scientists, and other students of decision-making processes. Adhering to this type (or close to it) are scholars who view the political scene as a clash of legitimate pressure groups with competing interests. For them, the main need today is to bring disparate interests together to achieve resolutions. More often than not, the best policy lies somewhere down the middle, with some accommodation of the paradigmatic jobs-versus-owls trade-off. Such scholars commonly concern themselves with inefficiencies and inconsistencies in the lawmaking process: too much red tape, too much litigation, policy decisions skewed by flawed decision-making processes and overly powerful pressure groups. Because of deficiencies such as these, statutes are not implemented as written, administrative decisions are sometimes in error, and appellate decisions go awry.

Scholars in the middle largely focus on the law as it is and try to make it better, taking note of environmental problems only to the extent that these are addressed in the law. Lots of basic legal work is done here: careful reading of texts, digging into legislative history, harmonizing inconsistent provisions, attacking bad reasoning, and blending one area of the law into other areas. Also drawing attention are the political processes of decision making, with talk about ways of getting citizens more involved and helping them understand better the issues being discussed. In some settings, market mechanisms are proposed for greater efficiency, but there is no dogmatic faith in the market. Cost-benefit analysis is mentioned often and favorably, and so is comparative risk analysis; though imperfect, both are viewed as sturdy staffs. Much writing has to do with the expanded use of negotiation methods and with tools for making complex data more comprehensible to ordinary people.

The fourth type group, the *progressive reformers,* comprises scholars most similar to the pioneers who instigated the great era of federal environmental lawmaking between the late 1960s and late 1970s—although they have now mellowed some, show more gray hair, and see the world more complexly. The aim for these scholars is to keep chipping away at key environmental problems, and they evaluate environmental laws and policies primarily by how successful they are in solving those problems. The progressive reformer is more likely to look outside existing law and processes, to read about underlying environmental issues, and to call for action to remedy those that the law addresses either poorly or not at all. The legal tools of choice vary, and keeping costs down and avoiding overregulation are preferred, in part so that more can get done. For the most part, the issues addressed by these scholars are the ones familiar to society at large, and they are commonly understood and described discretely. They chiefly have to do with direct threats to human health—things like pollution, toxic wastes, and now atmospheric problems—although they can also deal with endangered species, disappearing wildlands, and less familiar, more slow-developing problems.

The final type group, the *land community advocates,* is the most ecologically oriented. Scholars who embody or approach this ideal are the most worried about environmental problems and the most comprehensive in their understanding of them. Their chief focus is on issues that the law does not address. The pervasive sense is that grave environmental concerns are being addressed poorly, if at all. Although such scholars consider direct health threats to humans, even more troubling to them are the various forces that disrupt the healthy functioning of the entire land community—a community that includes soils, waters, plants, animals, and people. Along with the progressive reformers, scholars of this type are most closely linked to conservationists outside the field of law and most likely to work for public-interest conservation groups.

Land community advocates typically believe that environmental problems are deeply rooted in American culture. Quick fixes rarely work, they assert, and indeed often cause nearly as many difficulties as they solve. New technology that aims to cure the problems of the old technology often yields unexpected problems that are as bad or worse. Market solutions, intended to achieve greater efficiencies in resource use, can draw upon and exacerbate the very utilitarian, fragmented, ecologically uninformed view of nature that is a root cause of land degradation. Environmental ills, according to this scholarly type, are best understood as manifestations of underlying cultural problems, issues arising out of, and easily traced back to, the Enlightenment worldview with its reliance on reason and empirical data, its narrow moral and spiritual visions, and its unquestioned acceptance of human domination. Such scholars are likely to employ a broader perspective than scholars in other categories, and they are most apt to present issues in overtly moral terms. They also more frequently draw upon work from other scholarly disciplines, particularly history, environmental ethics, and sociology. At bottom, says the true land community advocate, conservation is not something that a society can buy or build. It is a matter of humility and discipline, an ethic that respects other life and future generations, a community orientation that favors quality over quantity and health over wealth.

We need to dig deeper than these quickly sketched categories to understand their differences. By and large, the variations among these scholarly types involve eight moral and intellectual issues.[5] On most of the issues, we can adequately survey the spectrum of views by identifying the two poles and taking selective note of the intermediate positions.

Human nature. Scholars differ widely today in how they understand the individual human and the human experience. Are humans best understood as autonomous individuals, or are they fundamentally social creatures? Are their understandings of the world, their values, and their perceptions individually formed, or are they rooted in and guided by tradition and surrounding social forces? Are people basically good when left alone and will they act responsibly, or do they act most responsibly in settings where they interact with others and are constrained by social norms? Are people able to achieve their goals acting alone and through entirely voluntary arrangements with others, or do they frequently need a more structured environment with decision making at the social or community level? Is there even such a thing as community, and does it make sense to talk about the well-being of the community as such?

In rough terms (and with a good deal of intermingling), libertarians are the most pronounced in their individualism; land community advocates are the most community focused. Libertarians readily allow individuals to pursue their self-interest and seek satisfaction of their self-selected preferences; along with the free market simple fixers, they are largely content to let people express their views as individuals acting alone and to let the market aggregate those views and translate them into policies. Land community advocates, on the other end of the spectrum, are apt to judge—and on occasion condemn—individual actions and preferences according to moral codes protective of the common life.

Libertarians are likely to portray individual preferences as autonomous choices, independently embraced by individuals acting as such. Land community advocates are contrarily prone to perceive such preferences as significantly shaped by social forces, including tradition, social norms, and (increasingly) aggressive advertising. They are likely, accordingly, to take a critical interest in the moral and ecological content of those social forces. They see knowledge as in large part a social construction and often view community wisdom as far greater than individual wisdom. They are also likely to note—and to place great emphasis on—the vastly different policy choices people make when acting as citizens rather than as consumers.

Libertarians commonly assume that individuals can adequately achieve their wants through voluntary means that respect the independence of all individuals. Land community advocates, in contrast, believe that many essential objectives are achievable only through collective and coercive action, including both landscape preservation goals (for example, wilderness area preservation and waterway management) and goals that require limits on destructive market competition (such as preserving soil on farmlands). As they see things, accordingly, a ban on coercive means effectively puts many environmental objectives out of reach. Focused on the community and desirous of community health, these conservationists call for decision-making processes that enable people collectively to get to know their lands, to learn about their problems, to exchange ethical and aesthetic preferences, and to make more healthful decisions about their collective fates.[6]

In the libertarian worldview, communities are chiefly aggregations of individuals and possess no real separate moral standing, nor are future generations owed any duties.[7] Land community advocates, in sharp contrast, see communities as vital structures deserving (and in many settings urgently needing) protection, and they view future generations as highly interested (if perforce silent) participants in current discussions. Both libertarians and land community advocates speak often about individual responsibility; they differ in that the latter perceive the individual's responsibilities as far more extensive.

Human place in nature. The first issue, views of human nature, blends into the second: how humans are understood in relation to nature.

For many scholars—those that embrace the dominant American ethic—humans stand apart from nature; humans hold a unique position among creatures, and the land is merely the place where they live.[8] Nature in this moral view is a collection of natural resources that humans may use at will. Some believe that we ought to conserve certain resources for future use by means of collective planning; others conclude that well-structured market mechanisms can manage the issue as well or better. In either case, there is little question that nature exists for human use and consumption. Because the land is merely a tool for humans to use, human dealings with it are best understood in utilitarian terms, with calculations properly focused on how various strategies directly affect humans. Because the land is well understood as a collection of resources, it is appropriate to divide it into pieces—legally, physically, and mentally—and to think about the parts individually. Fragmenting nature is particularly important to free market fixers, for a true market can work only if the market can move nature's pieces around, shifting them to their highest and best uses. In valuing nature's many parts, the market is the best guide, and market substitutes are useful in the case of parts that are not bought and sold.

On the other end of this issue, land community advocates (and to a lesser degree the progressive reformers) see the natural world far more complexly and holistically. Humans are not distinct from the rest of nature, ecologically or morally. As much as any organisms, humans are linked to the land, to the soil, waters, air, and other life forms.[9] The parts create a whole, however variable over time, and humans depend ultimately on the well-being of that whole. From this perspective, the landscape is an integrated community, and human-drawn boundaries are artificial and hence dangerous, however necessary or useful they might be in particular settings. The moral worldview embraced here stands in contrast to many of the dominant assumptions of modern culture, particularly American culture, which more than others has embraced individualism and framed important social issues in terms of individual rights, not the overall good. The anthropocentrism of values, the separation of humans from nature, the privileging of human reason over other ways of knowing, the tendency to base decisions on knowledge alone, the focus on the present, the acceptance of market valuations, and most of all the acquisitive individualism: all of these cultural elements are suspect, not because they are entirely wrong but because they are too powerful, too influential, and hence destructive.

Our knowledge of nature. A third difference regards our knowledge of nature and how we use that knowledge in our individual and collective lives. Here again, the land community advocates stand out from the other types in their belief that human knowledge is glaringly inadequate. Nature is more complex than people know and more complex then they probably can know (a common land-community expression). Science is important, and the gathering of more information is essential. But it is a mistake to think that this information can ever be more than a partial representation of the natural world.

This sense of human ignorance pervades the thought of land community advocates, and one of the chief challenges for scholars of this type is to find wise ways to deal with that ignorance. One way is to exercise caution and act humbly, to embrace what is sometimes called the precautionary principle.[10] Equally valuable is to draw upon nature's embedded wisdom, to tailor human ways to comply with nature's modes of operations, whether the task is growing food or fiber, managing rivers, or dealing with wastes. Because knowledge is incomplete, decision-making processes are inevitably flawed when they look solely to what is known. The known needs to be blended with the unknown, and that can occur only by drawing upon ethical values and mimicking nature's ways.[11]

For scholars at the other end of the typology spectrum, knowledge-based decision making is unproblematic. Indeed, there is often hostility to any decisions that are not based entirely on hard, verifiable facts. Decision-making processes are commonly slanted so people can act as they please, unless the proven facts show unmistakably that harm is occurring (scientific proof, loosely pegged at the 95 percent confidence level, is sometimes demanded). In the antithesis of the precautionary principle, the burden of proof is pushed to the opposite side. For technological fixers, the assumption is that good science can for the most part uncover all that we need to know, and the main need today is simply to get the missing information and put it to use. For free market fixers, on the other hand, current knowledge is good enough to make sound decisions and market forces provide adequate incentive to gain more knowledge. People acting alone are presumed to know what they need to know to live rightly in relation to nature (that is, to make rational decisions). When consumers enter the market and register their views with their dollars, they presumably know enough to make sound choices about their long-term well-being. Public policy is simply a matter of aggregating these individual choices.

Identification and understanding of environmental problems. Different burdens of proof, different epistemologies, and different perceptions of human nature help account for the widely varying understandings scholars have about current environmental problems. At one end of the spectrum are scholars who focus on direct, immediate impacts to human health, measured with the burden of proof sternly imposed on those who would claim problems. For libertarians and free market fixers, resource exhaustion is not a problem because the market can be counted on to find substitutes. Since nature is basically just a collection of resources, land degradation causes worry only when markets are askew. The only true environmental concern is with direct health effects on humans living today, and claims of adverse impacts, especially when coming from conservation groups, are typically judged with suspicion. Particularly for libertarians, the bigger issue today is not environmental degradation but overregulation and restrictions on individual liberty.

As one moves from the libertarian side toward the other, the burden of proof slowly lowers and the range of perceived problems increases. Ecological interconnections start to gain mention, and at some point the understanding is introduced that people are part of a complex, interconnected community and dependent on the well-being of that community. Attention begins to shift from problems considered in the law to those that are not. As the perspective lengthens in time, gradual, serious problems begin to surface, so much so that by the time one reaches the perspective of the land community advocates, the most severe environmental issues are ones that are hardly ever noted by libertarians and fixers. An array of issues relating to biological diversity rises toward the top, along with associated worries about genetic tampering, overuses of antibiotics and pesticides, and the spread of exotic species. In many parts of the country, soil-related issues take top billing as the greatest long-term concern. Issues like hydrologic modification, rarely mentioned on the libertarian end of the typology spectrum, break into the top five most severe problems for many land community advocates.

Ultimately, though, land community advocates do not view environmental problems as severable from the cultural and ethical deficiencies of modern society.[12] Specific environmental issues—water pollution, for instance—while obviously problems in themselves, are equally symptoms of an underlying malaise. They are the fever that provides evidence of the infection. The true problems have to do with human perceptions and values, with modern culture's infatuation with human reason and information, with excessive individualism of the acquisitive, irresponsible type, with human-centered value structures, and, most of all, with a cultural disconnection from the natural order.

Spatial and temporal scales of analysis. As scholars consider problems, they display remarkable variations in the temporal and spatial scales that they employ for analysis. This issue is one rarely remarked upon,[13] but along with burden-of-proof differences it probably accounts for a greater part of the variation in scholarly types than any other single factor.

When libertarians and free market fixers consider the best use of a parcel of land, they typically think of the particular parcel alone, as a discrete part of nature, just as they consider a water flow alone or a particular threatened species alone. They speak of its value as a distinct thing and of its potential highest and best use considered in isolation. On the other end of the spectrum, the tendency is to consider a broader scale, to look at the landscape or ecosystem as a whole and to consider individual resource-use issues in the context of the healthy functioning of that landscape. A part of nature is valued, not alone and apart, but in context, with due regard for its roles in sustaining the health and beauty of the community of life.

The spatial scale issue, however, is a tricky one, and it is a mistake to assume that one scholarly type always favors a small scale and another a larger one. Land community advocates examine problems from a variety of scales, with the aim of gaining the best understanding (as they see it) of the community's long-term well-being. Libertarian critics, on the other side, employ spatial scales that tend (and perhaps are intended) to discount alleged problems and to discredit the need for conservation proposals. Thus, we have libertarians claiming that a particular species, once widespread but now endangered, is adequately protected if it exists in even one location; that is, they assess the issue on a large spatial scale. Land community advocates, on the other side—worried as they are about the health of every neighborhood—mourn the species' absence from the many places that it no longer inhabits; for them, the fact that a species is alive somewhere on the planet doesn't help the small-scale health of a neighborhood where it is gone.

In terms of temporal scale, free market fixers nominally consider the future but subordinate it to present values. In practice, though, the future quite often is ignored except to the extent that individual consumers choose to let it affect their buying decisions. Libertarians are equally focused on the present, or rather equally willing to permit individuals living today to decide for themselves whether the future counts. At the land community end, issues like soil degradation loom large, even though effects may not be noticed for decades, generations, or even centuries. Land community advocates and progressive reformers alone seem to care that tree-farm practices are sustainable for only a few generations of trees; for other scholars, a few generations of trees is, as a policy matter, the same as forever.

Overall goals of conservation work and environmental law. It is on this issue, the overall goal of conservation, that the five scholarly types most visibly show their stripes. For libertarians, the goal of environmental law (meaning, for them, the law governing our interactions with nature) is to structure rules so that humans are allowed maximum individual freedom in their dealings with the land, consistent with equal freedom for others. For free market fixers, the goal is to get the prices right and otherwise correct market failures so that markets in nature adequately reflect relative resource values. For technological fixers, the focus is on promoting the best technology; otherwise, these scholars largely leave the work of goal setting to others. Here, as in other areas of law, dispute resolvers are out to find the compromise that gives every side a bit of what it wants. Progressive reformers, in turn, work to make incremental progress in remedying the obvious threats to human health and overt signs of land degradation. Finally, land community advocates seek to promote the long-term health and beauty of the entire land community. At one end of the scholarly spectrum, then, the focus is on mitigating direct, immediate impacts to the health of humans living today while at the other, it is chiefly on the community and on the long term, with special recognition of future generations and other life forms.

Of all the scholarly types, progressive reformers are most apt to see the law as a potent tool in bringing about environmental gains. Land community advocates are typically more pessimistic, sometimes so much so that they see wrangling about laws and formal law-making processes as diversionary if not wasteful. If environmental degradation stems from social and culture deficiencies, then those deficiencies need to be addressed directly. To change laws without changing society is to produce merely a facade of progress. According to the true land community advocate, people need to think more ecologically and recognize their ultimate dependence on a healthy land; they need to embrace better values, particularly greater humility; they need to admit and act upon the limits of human knowledge and reasoning; perhaps above all, they need to love the land more and feel greater emotional attachment to it. According to this type, the law is a weak tool to bring about such growth.

History and environmental progress. Because they take the longest-term view and because they see environmental problems as having deep historical roots, land community advocates show the most interest in history. Environmental history, in fact, is one of the primary nonlegal disciplines they use. Few others see much value in history, although free market fixers sometimes offer their own versions of history. In the free market story, history tends to comply with (or to be aptly summarized by) rather simple neoclassical economic theories. Economic forces and unrestrained enterprise account for essentially all progress. In this view, environmental improvement occurs more or less invisibly as a country gets more wealthy, which means that the key to improving the environment in a country is to increase its wealth. Land community advocates, in sharp contrast, see environmental progress as largely stemming not from the market but from democratic restraints on the market. Indeed, the entire environmental movement,[14] which is given credit for much of the improvement that has occurred, is viewed principally as a much-needed reaction to the destruction wrought by a free market. For this type, economic growth might be *correlated* with environmental improvement (ignoring for this purpose ecological declines and environmental costs shifted overseas), but the *causation* largely works in the opposite direction.

Land community advocates pay particular attention to the evolution of values and institutions over time. In that history of change, in that record of cultural growth, lies their hope that environmental ills in time might lessen. From their institutional study of private property, for instance, they conclude that ownership norms have shifted significantly over time. Definitions of land-use "harm" have been malleable, cultural creations, reshaped in response to evolving conditions and values. That record of change offers hope to this type that property norms one day might reflect, far better than they now do, the limits that nature imposes on sound land use. Focusing by necessity on the long term, land community advocates hold out the hope that humans one day might embrace a humble, religiously oriented understanding of the precarious human predicament.

Role of the imagination. In terms of imagining how the land might be better, the dispute resolvers in the middle have very little other than a vision of widespread social consensus. Libertarians cherish the vision of a society populated by individuals who, on their own, choose to live responsibly and are given freedom to do so. Free market fixers look forward to an endless unfolding process of greater economic growth; how that growth might occur, in terms of the particular goods and services that a market generates, is presumably of little interest. Progressive reformers look instead to a lessening of particular environmental ills so that people can live more healthful lives with ample opportunities to interact with nature. Land community advocates dream of a time when the land waxes in its natural health and when people are more aware of it and attached to it. They think not just of clean air and water but of farm fields that build soil rather than lose it, of rivers with water flows that are largely natural, and of forests that are true biological communities rather than monocultural farms.

When it began in earnest, scholarship about environmental law and public policy was a distinctly value-driven enterprise, as conservation biology is today. That characteristic has become less evident, as fewer and fewer scholars display passion about environmental ills. Within the profession of practicing lawyers, the change is even more evident. Indeed, an "environmental lawyer," as often as not, is now someone engaged in helping polluters and land developers diminish their environmental responsibilities. Environmental law is merely another field of practice-for-hire, not a value-driven effort to craft more enduring, satisfying ways to live in nature.

Money accounts for part of this shift; defending polluters is far more profitable and there is more work to be had. Then, too, self-interest and even greed have resurfaced as more respectable values, particularly in libertarian writing. But the principal cause probably lies in the greater complexity of issues today. No sane person a generation ago spoke in favor of flaming rivers and fields filled with dead songbirds. Today, no environmental issue goes unchallenged by defenders of the status quo. In truth, polluters know the benefits of public relations, and they can easily outspend citizen watchdog groups. They know, too, the benefits of generating scientific and economic studies that support their positions—or at least that confuse an issue enough to create the two-sides-to-the-question policy clash that journalists find convenient. Yet, even aside from such smoke screens, issues have in fact become more complex, particularly in the case of problems that are long term or that affect humans in ways that seem remote to ordinary citizens. Good work has become necessary—not just good science and good economics but good philosophy, good social and political criticism, good history, and just plain good thought and feeling.

Too often today's readers of scholarly journals are required to fill in the background gaps in the scholarly presentations, and they are left confused by what they read. The points that scholars directly address are important enough. But scholarly debates are often weakly joined, if joined at all, because the true disagreements are deeper and on points not overtly raised. So we see, to use merely one example, disputes among legal scholars about regulatory "takings" and private property rights that have little or nothing to do with the superficial issue being discussed—how much protection property should receive—and far more to do with ecological perceptions, burdens of proof, views of humans as individuals versus community members, short-term versus long-term scales of analysis, the perceived cultural roots of degradation, the extent of human knowledge about nature, and the like. Disputes over free trade and market-based environmental policies are also rarely joined, and for similar reasons. Here, too, we have unstated disputes about whether humans are or are not appropriately viewed as autonomous, mobile individuals, disconnected from any place and not properly concerned about the health of any place. We have unvoiced assumptions about how environmental progress occurs, whether by community study and action and restraints on the market or whether by simple economic growth. We have disagreements about whether it is useful or hurtful to strengthen perceptions about nature as a warehouse of natural resources, available for humans to tap.

Many authors avoid background issues by assuming the posture of the detached, scholarly technician, devoted to remedying problems—much like the automobile mechanic who takes on a sputtering carburetor. The results of this approach are too often unsatisfying, producing fragmented scholarly fields in a wide array of policy subfields. Small pockets of scholars speak to one another, but the scholarly community as a whole often does not. Indeed, it hardly has much ground to interact, given the distance among many scholars before their opening sentences are written, let alone read. Surely our work would improve collectively if we stepped back and talked more about the earlier parts of our stories, if we talked more about our intellectual and moral paths. It is along those paths where our real differences are to be found.

One benefit of talking more about underlying assumptions is that we're likely to understand them better ourselves. To talk about them, we need first to identify them and think about them, deeply and professionally. To do that, we need to explore the extensive literature written about them. At the least, we need to state our assumptions more overtly, noting our reliance on them, so that our conclusions can be viewed as they ought to be: as conditional conclusions, conditioned upon value assumptions that are debatable and that very much need debating.

In a thoughtful study of environmental law scholarship, Richard Lazarus has highlighted some of the challenges that confront scholars first wading into environmental law.[15] The statutes are numerous, complex, inconsistent, and just plain poorly written. Regulations are voluminous and every bit as contorted. Law in the field is far different from law on the books. Then there is the scientific complexity of it all and the infusion of complex economic jargon. Not surprisingly, Lazarus relates, many legal scholars skirt the field by addressing instead issues of environmental federalism, environmental justice, or administrative process—topics that require far less mastery of the environmental literature.

The complexity of the field, though, is even greater than Professor Lazarus allows, for the tribulations he mentions are all within environmental law as a distinct element of conservation policy. To think seriously about background issues such as overall aims and ultimate causes—which legal scholars need to do, just as much as other environmental policy specialists—is to add whole new layers of complexity. The literature on these background issues is hardly less vast than it is on strictly legal subjects. Included here are not just the foundational, growing literatures of conservation biology, environmental philosophy, environmental history, and communitarian social policy but the poetry, essays, and fiction of Wendell Berry; the agriculture writings of Wes Jackson, Gene Logsdon, and David Kline; the cultural critiques of Lewis Mumford, Christopher Lasch, David Ehrenfeld, John Ralston Saul, and David Orr; the cultural forays of Gary Nabhan, Evan Eisenberg, Bill McKibben, Ted Williams, and Stephanie Mills; the community-based writings of Alan Durning and Scott Russell Sanders; the meditations on Western lands by Wallace Stegner, Gretel Ehrlich, Patricia Limerick, Richard Manning, and Charles Wilkinson; and even such literary works as *Cold Mountain,* Charles Frazier's engaging exploration of nature and culture.

No scholar, of course, has time to read everything pertinent, nor is there need to redo work already done well by others; a division of labor is as useful as it is necessary. But it is one thing to divide up the tasks, leaving others to grapple with fundamental questions of value and direction, and something far different to charge ahead with little sense of direction, ignoring the issues and unaware of the literature.

Good scholarship is necessarily written with a clear understanding of where conservation work needs to head. Thus, a sound sense of ultimate aims is necessary for nearly everyone. It is not enough, for instance, to put neoclassical economic policy models to use, as if they were value free or enjoyed unquestioned scholarly acceptance; they are not and do not. Nor is it enough to embrace a goal such as sustainability, at least without specifying clearly what the term means and how it fits into the long-term ecological functioning of natural communities. (See chapter 4 for my fuller criticism of sustainability.) The same can be said about the use of biodiversity indicators as measures of good land use; they are ecologically vital but tell us little about how lands can best serve human needs. A different problem arises in the work of scholars who dwell upon alternative policy means without ever stopping to think clearly about the desired ends. With no ends in sight, how can one judge the effectiveness of alternative means?

Katherine Anne Porter may have begun "Jilting" with Mrs. Weatherall on her deathbed, but we can be sure that before beginning to write her tale, she knew all about Granny's life and struggles. She knew, that is, Granny's exact path to her final scene. And while Porter gives us only pieces and hints about that path, it is enough for us to make substantial progress in reconstructing it. As readers, we know from the opening paragraph that we are entering a tale close to its end, so we are alert for background clues.

Good environmental writing can be crafted in just this way; it, too, can begin close to the key conflict. But it can begin like this only when the author, like Ms. Porter, has carefully thought out the path and gives readers enough clues to reconstruct the essential parts of it. Undue repetition always presents a trade-off, and good writings are kept succinct. But current scholarship cries out for more attention to the fundamentals.

CHAPTER 3

The Lure of the Garden

R ecent public talk about land conservation has featured prominently, if not been dominated by, several different contentions that we can reasonably achieve our land-related environmental goals if only we embrace some simple measure or particular policy idea. Most notable of these has been the claim that land conservation will come about, to the extent that it makes good sense, when all parts of nature are privatized—that is, turned into secure private property. Related to this is the claim that conservation will take place, again to the degree that is most sound, when the market is fully unleashed and when every part of nature is subject to it, thereby allowing market forces to move nature's parts to their highest and best uses. Less sweeping than these is a third, equally simple proffered solution: that conservation would happen if we revised the ways we think about land and human life on it—if we simply viewed the land as a garden, and then worked to make it more beautiful and productive.[1]

Privatization and market-based solutions have drawn warmest support from business groups and antigovernment ideologues (the Heritage Foundation, CATO Institute, American Enterprise Institute) that display little real interest in healthy lands. The tend-the-garden line of thought, in contrast, has come from conservationists who believe their cause has gone astray in its ethics, aesthetics, and overreliance on ecological science.

Tend-the-garden thinking gained ground in the early 1990s, largely arising from the conflict between conservation and the rising backlash against environmentalism. That backlash included several cultural components: the "wise-use" movement, which sought to intensify extractive uses of publicly owned resources (mining, timber harvesting, irrigation); the "property rights" movement, which defended intensive uses of private lands; and the growing criticism of government generally, influenced by libertarian and free market ideology. Backlash rhetoric portrayed environmentalists as zealots or close to it. They were misanthropes who cared about every life form except humans. Out to lock up as much land as possible, they were driven by a religious paganism that deserved no role in the democratic arena.[2]

A consistent weakness in backlash rhetoric has been its lack of citations to specific organizations, people, or writings. Charges leveled against "radical environmentalists" or ardent "preservationists" were rarely connected to any platforms, organizations, or well-known figures. To observers who really knew conservation, the charges seemed greatly miscast, save as applied to a few individuals at the outer fringe of the conservation bell curve. (They overlooked, for instance, the massive conservation effort aimed at providing clean air to breathe, clean water to drink, healthy food to eat, and natural areas to visit.) Still, the image of the zealous environmentalist appeared plausible, particularly in anecdotal tales about misguided land-use rules. It took hold as a broad and powerful condemnation.

If radical environmentalism as thus defined provided the social thesis, and the wise-use and property rights movements arose as the antitheses, it was only a matter of time before a synthesis emerged, a line of thought that expressed care for the land but that rejected the zeal attributed to radicals on both sides. The synthesis claimed to stand at the middle of things, at the "radical center" of thinking about land—the place where people of balanced judgment should properly end up.

Biologist René Dubos offered an early version of this tend-the-garden reasoning in his prominent work from 1980, *The Wooing of Earth*.[3] Dubos celebrated the human capacity to improve nature when people exercised their aesthetic imaginations and used the land with respect and love. A more pointed, revealing example of this thought appeared in 1991, in the book *Second Nature* by Michael Pollan, a *Harper's* editor who spent eight years living in Connecticut tending a backyard garden.[4] *Second Nature* recorded Pollan's trial-and-error education as he gradually turned his spacious yard over to vegetables, fruit trees, and ornamental plantings. Woven among his garden exploits were critical comments about the environmentalism of the day and suggestions on redirecting it. His own garden experiences, Pollan asserted, illustrated the path to a more wholesome bond between people and land. To tend a garden well, fostering its beauty, was to enact on a small scale what humanity needed to do on the Earth generally. Pollan's book was an early leading work in this genre of conservation thought, helping to set the tone for much that followed.

A good way to probe this tend-the-garden line of thought, seeing what it contains and gauging its strengths, is to compare Pollan's *Second Nature* with a 1939 essay by Aldo Leopold, "The Farmer as a Conservationist."[5] In his work, half a century earlier than Pollan's, Leopold also offered readers a vivid image of how private lands conservation might be achieved.[6] Pollan in his 1990s vision described a backyard gardener-cum-conservationist who tilled his soil to produce food and flowers. Years earlier, Leopold used the same literary technique to the same end; his farmer, like Pollan's gardener, exemplified the attitudes and practices that humanity needed to embrace if land and people were to thrive.

Leopold wrote "The Farmer as a Conservationist" for a general audience, principally farm readers. His purpose in writing it was the same one that led him a few years later to assemble the pieces in *A Sand County Almanac:* to encourage landowners to practice conservation and to illustrate the value of protecting private lands. By 1939 Leopold understood that government alone could not remedy the conservation challenges of the day, particularly in landscapes where public lands were few and private farms intensively used. In such a working landscape, conservation required action by individual owners. One by one, landowners needed to leave room for wild plants and animals, to care for the soil, and to restore natural water flows.

Leopold's essay and Pollan's book display striking parallels. Both authors had in mind two principal reading audiences: a primary audience of landowners, whom they presumably hoped would accept and act upon their land-use advice, and a more general audience of readers who were interested in conservation but needed guidance to think about it clearly. The works are similar also in that both authors criticized dominant modes of thought, not just the ideas of people willing to abuse land but also those of well-meaning conservationists whose work was simply not well aimed.

How, then, does the tend-the-garden line of conservation thought compare with Leopold's "The Farmer as a Conservationist," and what light does the comparison shed on where we stand today?

Leopold's essay is the shorter of the two works, but Leopold knew how to pack big ideas into small packages. "Conservation," he announced plainly in the essay's first line, "means harmony between men and land." "When land does well for its owner, and the owner does well by his land; when both end up better by reason of their partnership, we have conservation. When one or the other grows poorer, we do not" (255).

Properly undertaken, Leopold implied, conservation could achieve a desirable outcome for people and land alike. Thus, dealings with the land were best understood not as adversarial or unequal but as a partnership for the benefit of all. To call this relationship a partnership implied a certain mutuality and reciprocal respect, a need for cooperation and give-and-take. By describing the human-land bond in this way, Leopold introduced the ecological orientation that was so central to his views. People belonged to the land just as much as the land belonged to people. All life that inhabited a place, people included, formed an integrated community of life. Like other communities, the land community could be more or less healthy and prosperous.

Land degradation took place, Leopold explained, not only when people exhausted the land by using it too intensively but when the land's mechanisms got out of order. Conservation, accordingly, was about "keeping the resource in working order, as well as preventing overuse" (257). In many instances of degradation, land remained fertile yet its inner workings had become disrupted, just as the inner workings of a machine might fail if it were missing parts or drained of oil. Leopold's farm audience knew all about machines and what it took to keep them functioning. To this audience it was rhetorically effective to speak of the land as a mechanism, even though Leopold knew the comparison was imprecise. As for farmland, it got out of order when livestock grazed in woodlots, when waterways were unduly drained or straightened, and when soil was so abused that it no longer performed its physical and biological functions.

Leopold's ecological message made the work of conservation more difficult because it required landowners to understand their farms as integrated ecosystems. They had to learn to spot evidence of malfunctioning so they could act to correct it. Leopold's message also required landowners to pay attention to all of nature's parts, even those that seemed worthless to humans, because innumerable parts helped sustain the land's operation. Here Leopold offered as example the bog-birch, "a mousy, unobtrusive, inconspicuous, uninteresting little bush" (261) that met no human need for food or fiber. What the bog-birch did do was supply needed food for the sharp-tailed grouse and other wildlife during difficult winter months. It kept wildlife from starving, with the wildlife, in turn, playing important roles in keeping the land machine humming along.

At this point, Leopold was close to the heart of things. To practice conservation, landowners needed to know a great deal, and they needed the ability to use that knowledge in a hands-on way. Leopold referred to this knowledge base simply as "skill," a talent, he said, that could not be learned from books alone. Skill came from a careful attentiveness to the land and from a readiness to respect nature's equal management role. Skill arose within a person who possessed "a lively and vital curiosity about the workings of the biological engine," a person inspired by "enthusiasm and affection." These were "the human qualities requisite to better land use" (258).

So what kinds of land-use decisions would such a skilled person make, Leopold asked, and what would the land then look like? Here Leopold was brief because he believed specific answers depended on the land itself. In southern Wisconsin, a skilled farmer would certainly "devote land to woods, marsh, pond, [and] windbreaks" as well as to row crops and pasture. He would commit land to bushy fencerows for birds and leave snag trees for raccoons. He would also, Leopold hoped, leave space "for a patch of ladyslippers, a remnant of prairie, or just scenery." Many of these moves, he confessed, made no money for the landowner. They were valuable only in the sense that they made the land more enjoyable and helped promote its health (263–64).

If all landowners possessed what Leopold called skill and if they followed through on the conservation practices he recommended, the land would have "a certain wholeness." Leopold described this wholeness by comparing land with the human body: "No one censures a man who loses his leg in an accident, or who was born with only four fingers, but we should look askance at a man who amputated a natural part on the grounds that some other is more profitable. The comparison is exaggerated; we had to amputate many marshes, ponds and woods to make the land habitable, but to remove any natural feature from representation in the rural landscape seems to me a defacement which the calm verdict of history will not approve, either as good conservation, good taste, or good farming" (259).

Leopold envisioned a landscape in which people made room for other life forms. "Doesn't conservation imply a certain interspersion of land-uses," he asked rhetorically, "a certain pepper-and-salt pattern in the warp and woof of the land-use fabric"? If so, then landowners had no choice but to be conservationists. "It is the individual farmer who must weave the greater part of the rug on which America stands. Shall he weave into it only the sober yarns which warm the feet, or also some of the colors which warm the eye and the heart?" (260) This question, Leopold believed, was one for farmers themselves to answer. But they were not therefore private decisions to which neighbors and other community members would be indifferent. "The landscape of any farm is the owner's portrait of himself" (263). What a person did on the land told the whole world the kind of person he was, about his level of skill, his concern for aesthetics and future generations, and his willingness to help shoulder communal burdens.

One obstacle to the achievement of a healthy landscape was the adverse economic effects of conservation for the farmer acting alone. But lying behind economic realities was a way of thinking about land that propelled people to degrade what they possessed. "Sometimes I think that ideas, like men, can become dictators," Leopold wrote, as the world was once again slipping into war: "We Americans have so far escaped regimentation by our rulers, but have we escaped regimentation by our own ideas? I doubt if there exists today a more complete regimentation of the human mind than that accomplished by our self-imposed doctrine of ruthless utilitarianism. The saving grace of democracy is that we fastened this yoke on our own necks, and we can cast it off when we want to, without severing the neck. Conservation is perhaps one of the many squirmings which foreshadow this act of self-liberation" (259).

Having chastised his readers, Leopold ended his essay with a carrot—an alluring vision of what the future could hold if his ideas took root. What might a corn-belt farm look like, Leopold wondered aloud, after years of attentive conservation? There is the creek that would be unstraightened, he noted, with its banks wooded and ungrazed. The woodlot, also ungrazed, would include young sprouts as well as "a sprinkling of hollow-limbed veterans," and around the edge a few "widespreading hickories and walnuts for nutting." "Many things are expected," Leopold related, "of this creek and its woods: cordwood, posts, and sawlogs; flood-control, fishing, and swimming; nuts and wildflowers; fur and feather. Should it fail to yield an owl-hoot or a mess of quail on demand, or a bunch of sweet william or a coon-hunt in season, the matter will be cause for injured pride and family scrutiny, like a check marked 'no funds'" (263). "The fields and pastures of this farm," Leopold continued, "like its sons and daughters, are a mixture of wild and tame attributes, all built on a foundation of good health. The health of the fields is their fertility. . . . The farmer is proud that all his soil graphs point upward, that he has no check dams or terraces, and needs none.

He speaks sympathetically of his neighbor who has the misfortune of harboring a gully, and who was forced to call in the CCC. The neighbor's check dams are a regrettable badge of awkward conduct, like a crutch" (263–64).

Leopold added still more detail to his idyllic vision of a healthy land. There was the bushy fencerow teeming with wildlife, the historic oaks, the prairie flowers and wild fruits, the bird list for the farm that included 161 species, and finally the farm pond, the "farmer's special badge of distinction," partially fenced off to protect ducks, rails, redwings, gallinules, and muskrats, provider of water lilies in September, good skating in winter, and rat pelts for "the boy's pin-money" (264).

With this argument and image, Leopold distilled his message to the landowner, the results of his personal effort to determine why bad land use was so common and what steps were required to correct it. This particularized vision of the individual farm, in turn, fit into Leopold's larger conservation agenda, which included healthy rivers, ample wildlife habitat, and well-chosen, diverse samples of wild areas. Unifying it all was the ideal of land health, proposed by Leopold as conservation's overall vision. Not all American land was farmland, and conservation involved more than just sound farm operations. But if America did not use its rural working lands correctly, conservation would never succeed.

In *Second Nature*, Michael Pollan situates his own garden image, and the conservation wisdom that he connects to it, boldly and powerfully. Pollan's image of man in the garden, tending the land with care, is proposed as a moderate alternative between two orientations toward the natural world that are, in Pollan's view, equally extreme. At one pole is the American inclination to dominate nature fully, to treat land as an object that humans can manipulate and consume at will. This attitude, Pollan relates, shows up emblematically in the standard American approach to lawns. Americans drench their lawns in chemicals to eliminate every plant and insect they do not like while cutting the grass itself to give a uniform, carpetlike appearance. The typical American does not interact with a lawn in a respectful way: he or she beats it with chemicals and machines to keep it in line.

At the other pole for Pollan are the radical environmentalists and naturalists who dislike any human alteration of nature and who are at root "indifferent to our well-being and survival as a species." ("Have you ever noticed," Pollan asks, "that the naturalist never tells you where he lives?" [58–59]) In the environmental worldview, according to Pollan, individual trees (and perhaps other plants) have rights, and people who protect forests do so to honor those individual rights (203–5). Environmentalists urge humans to replace their anthropocentrism with a biocentric ethic in which all species are equal. Driven by such moral impulses, environmentalists have little or no sense of the land's beauty; indeed, Pollan asserts, they are prone by their moral fervor to favor a hands-off attitude that produces landscapes that sensible people would deem ugly.

Pollan illustrates his environmental critique by recounting the story of Cathedral Pines, a forty-two-acre forest tract in New England owned by the Nature Conservancy that suffered severe wind damage in a storm (209–25). The Nature Conservancy was content to leave the tract alone but under pressure from local residents cut a firebreak around the tract's edge to reduce the chance of a spreading fire. The resulting landscape, Pollan says, was "grotesque" (238) because the conflicting worldviews that guided the forest's restoration were both misguided—on one side the ethic of domination, which Pollan attributes to the neighboring landowners (who wanted the ugly mess cleaned up and the whole forest replanted) and on the other side the wilderness ethic, which Pollan links to the Nature Conservancy (which proposed to leave the downed trees alone). It was "a classic environmental battle," in Pollan's interpretation, one that "seemed to exemplify just about everything that's wrong with the way we approach problems of this kind these days. . . . We should probably not be surprised," he observes, "that the result of such a confrontation is not a wilderness, or a garden, but a DMZ" (211, 238).

Pollan believes that we would be wiser to follow a middle path in our dealing with nature—between the chemically washed lawn and the worshiped wilderness, between complete domination and complete acquiescence. And the garden, he suggests, provides a clear vision of that path. "The idea of the garden—as a place, both real and metaphorical, where nature and culture can be wedded in a way that can benefit both—may be as useful to us today as the idea of wilderness has been in the past" (6). The garden "is a middle ground between nature and culture, a place that is at once of nature and unapologetically set against it" (64).

As Pollan sees things, gardeners are people who manipulate nature to produce the results they like. They are unafraid to favor some species over others and to focus solely on their personal needs and wants, yet their work is tempered by a measure of restraint. Gardeners undertake not to dominate nature completely but to achieve their production and aesthetic goals without using excessive force. A good gardener, that is, "can nimbly walk the line between the dangers of over- and undercultivation, between pushing nature too far and giving her too much ground" (148). Pollan envisions a kind of honest conflict on the land, the sort of battle that an honorable soldier might engage in, avoiding the equivalent of poison gas and taking no unfair advantage but nonetheless fighting with determination, skill, and a commitment to win.

Pollan's guiding idea, borrowed from Wendell Berry, is that humans ought to use nature as their measure, letting it guide them in their manipulations. ("Learn to think like running water, or a carrot, an aphid, a pine forest, or a compost pile," he urges, though all the while remembering that a garden ethic is "frankly anthropocentric" [232, 227].) Unlike Berry, however, Pollan seems confident that a skilled gardener can tease nature into providing humankind with limitless bounty. Nature really poses no limits, Pollan believes. Indeed, environmentalists who speak of such limits simply do not understand that the Earth is an open system, receiving inputs of sunlight daily. With such sunlight, everything is possible; "in terms of the global ecosystem, there is a free lunch and its name is photosynthesis." A good gardener can actually reverse the second law of thermodynamics, as Pollan has done in his own backyard. Our environmental problems, he asserts, "have more to do with our technologies and our habits and economic arrangements than with the planet's inherent limits or the burden of our numbers" (173).

What we require to move ahead, Pollan concludes, are new metaphors or images of nature. He derives several from his experiences looking at the trees of Connecticut. We should view nature, he says, as an organism, with the trees as its lungs that help clean the air. In addition, given global climate change and other atmospheric problems, we might properly view trees like the coal miner's canary. "It's obviously impossible to predict," Pollan says, but one can hope that these "new" metaphors will catch on (206).

When the garden supplies our image, Pollan explains, one's work with the land is guided by aesthetics and ethics. Aesthetics enters the management equation not to shed light on right and wrong conduct but to help construct a landscape that is more pleasing to the gardener. Free to implement his or her aesthetic preferences, Pollan's gardener can reshape things as he or she sees fit, replacing native species with highly bred ones and otherwise treating the land as a canvas awaiting the artist's touch. It is on the issue of aesthetics, Pollan asserts, that radical environmentalists are most plainly misguided. As evidence, he relates the tale of a prominent local environmentalist who put a compost pile in the middle of his garden. Pollan knows why this was done without even asking his neighbor: it was a moral gesture, devoid of a sense of aesthetics. Had the environmentalist let aesthetics be his guide, he presumably would have put a statue, small pool, or sundial in the middle (272–73).[7]

Pollan is vague on the ethics component of his land-management formula, but he manifests in his own work a distinct element of restraint and humility as he goes about refashioning nature. Pollan dislikes chemical pesticides and thinks a good gardener ought to compost. He chooses to leave the small wetland on his property undrained, although without explaining why he has done so or whether a gardener in his situation should feel obligated to do so. What Pollan offers, then–like René Dubos in his 1980 essay—is a suggestive rather than definitive vision of what good land use entails: "The gardener in nature is that most artificial of creatures, a civilized being: in control of his appetites, solicitous of nature, self-conscious and responsible, mindful of the past and the future, and at ease with the fundamental ambiguity of his predicament—which is that though he lives in nature, he is no longer strictly *of* nature. Further, he knows that neither his success nor his failure in this place is ordained. Nature is apparently indifferent to his fate, and this leaves him free—indeed, obliges him—to make his own way here as best he can" (232–33).

Pollan offers his garden vision as an all-encompassing conservation ethic, applicable, it seems (with appropriate adjustments) to all lands everywhere. When all lands are worked as gardens, we have no need for refuges or wild area set-asides. All acres are available to tend.

Pollan's book has gained admirers in large part because of his garden image—an image that (to the pleasure, no doubt, of many readers) puts humans firmly in the center and in control. It is essential in assessing his work to consider that garden image, both on its own and in comparison with Leopold's essay. Before such discussion, however, it is useful to assess a few of the less important but nonetheless instructive elements of Pollan's narrative.

A number of Pollan's comments about environmentalists are plainly more literary caricature than accurate description, taken not from real life but from depictions constructed by the backlash against environmentalism. They describe no sizeable element within the turn-of-the-century conservation movement, nor does Pollan offer evidence supporting his claims. One is hard-pressed, for instance, to find evidence of any assertion that individual trees as such have rights, a view that for Pollan characterizes environmental thought as a whole (though there are many who believe, as did Albert Schweitzer, that all life deserves a modicum of respect—but that is a claim quite distant from the assertion of "rights" for individual plants) (203).[8] Pollan's complaint that environmentalism is driven by a vision of untouched wilderness is also wide of the mark, though it does bring in a tiny strand of the movement. The truth is that conservation has always centered on mitigating direct insults to human health (mostly pollution and toxic contaminants) and on improving the condition of places where people live, the air they breathe, the water they drink, and the food they eat.[9] Such efforts dominate day-to-day conservation work everywhere; in some areas they make up the totality of it. Wilderness preservation is only a small part of the overall picture.

Even wilderness protection efforts (which Pollan does support) have commonly drawn justification from the many ways that wild patches aid larger, human-inhabited landscapes along with the direct values of such places for human users.[10] Efforts to protect endangered species have similarly been phrased in terms of the values such species have or might have for humans—more often than in the biocentric rhetoric that Pollan condemns. Indeed, many conservationists complain because species preservation efforts are *not* more focused on the perceived moral duties of humans now living to protect other species (duties owed either to the species themselves or to future human generations). According to public opinion surveys, such moral claims are supported by over 80 percent of all Americans, with the public as a whole supporting them more strongly even than members of the Sierra Club.[11] Aside from their lack of factual support, Pollan's allegations of indifference to human well-being could easily insult a good many community-minded conservationists.

Pollan is certainly right that environmentalists view human culture as the ultimate origin of our problems. But then so do environmental historians, virtually all scholars who have probed the issue, and even the public at large. Flawed culture is at the heart of environmental decline. Environmentalists have striven for years to highlight these flaws, just as Pollan himself does.

Pollan's work is weakened by his straw-man (albeit entertaining) constructions of environmental thought. Such pejorative constructions, however, serve merely as backdrop to his own vision of humans active in the garden. That image, a more positive and well-considered offering, deserves a close look.

When the gardener begins creating a garden, the first step is typically to strip the land clean, just as Pollan did on much of his own Connecticut land. Plow under everything that is there and start anew. What will be planted is chosen by the gardener; it is a human choice, guided by the gardener's preferences and wants. Nature, of course, constrains the gardener by allowing only certain species to grow outdoors in a given climate. But in Pollan's scheme that is apparently nature's only role. Pollan is content to allow garden space for nonnative plants, whether from across the continent or from around the world. He is also content to install plants that can live only with constant human attention; their natural vigor or hardiness is of no particular concern. Indeed, he seems to like the idea that in a garden everything depends on the gardener and will die if he or she fails to tend the place well (267).

In Pollan's garden only his few chosen species are welcome, and he vigorously wards off other plants and animals. Pollan does show restraint in his chosen means of attacking pests, favoring biological controls over chemical ones. But it is not clear why that is so nor whether his garden image would necessarily lead to such restraint, morally or ecologically. The line Pollan draws around his garden—chosen species in, unwanted ones out—is emblematic of the ecological disconnection between Pollan's garden and surrounding nature. Inputs, for both the garden and the gardener, arrive from somewhere else, and wastes largely go somewhere out of sight. It is a linear system, just like that of industrial agriculture, not the cyclical fertility system that characterizes nature left alone.

Pollan's personal garden happens to abut wooded land and perhaps comports well enough with the ecological health of the larger landscape (though Pollan scoffs at the connection: "don't lecture me about . . . the continuity of gardens and the natural landscape" [58]). But what if his situation had been otherwise? What if his garden had abutted a neighbor's garden, and that one abutted another, and each gardener kept out unwanted species and paid no attention to ecological interconnections? What if his garden were like an Illinois cornfield, side by side with other cornfields and intensively managed so that disfavored species (that is, virtually all species) had no places to live? Where would the landscape be, biologically speaking?

At bottom, Pollan's garden is merely an arbitrary patch in a much larger landscape, more the product of surveyors' lines than any sensitivity to nature. It is a separate piece of the land under the gardener's complete control. Focused on the small piece of land, the gardener can easily ignore the ecological ripples. The underlying problem here, most simply, is Pollan's small spatial scale. The gardener's concern is with the productivity and beauty of the patch alone, not the larger landscape. Then there is the related problem of the gardener's isolation from the surrounding social world. Pollan positively encourages gardeners to embrace a go-it-alone attitude. Put up a wall or fence around the garden, he recommends, so that no one can look in and so that you can do what you want, free of outside pressure (60, 271). In dealing with surrounding landowners, the best attitude, we are told, is the American liberal ideal of live and let live–precisely the attitude that has brought so much destruction.

Pollan suggests that aesthetics will prompt a gardener to take decent care of the land, but beauty untethered from nature is notoriously subjective. The farmer who keeps bean fields weed free with herbicides, the rural landowner who mows acres of lawn and leaves room for nothing but grass, the pond owner who puts rocks all around the water's edge and excludes all nesting vegetation for waterfowl, the landowner who cuts down dead trees because they are unsightly—for all of this, perceived beauty is a motivating force. As for Pollan's own personal aesthetic sense, he is fond of geometric patterns and is particularly drawn to straight lines: "I immediately liked the way a freshly cultivated row of plants stood out against the rolling land around it, the stillness of it in the face of so much upheaval. That rub, between the flat manmade line and the landscape's own bent toward curve and motion, seems to lend a certain energizing tension to a garden, to give it, quite literally, an edge" (287).[12]

For his most extended example of how to meld nature and culture without overcultivation, Pollan turns to his rose beds and to the vast rose-breeding industry. In doing so, though, he succeeds far better in entertaining readers than in clarifying his conservation scheme. Pollan prefers older rose varieties, which are more disease resistant and more fragrant. A particular favorite is the Madame Hardy rose, which first appeared in 1832. It "embodies the classic form of old roses, and comes closer to the image the word rose has conjured up in people's minds . . . than does the rose in our florist shops today" (108). Contrasted with the Madame Hardy is the contemporary, showy Dolly Parton rose ("a rose with, you have guessed it, exceptionally large blossoms" [97–98]). The Madame Hardy rose is a good product of nature and culture coming together; the Dolly Parton, in contrast, is a "regrettable offspring" (113). Our prime need today, Pollan tells us—more important even than protecting swamps—is "to learn how to mingle our art with nature in ways that culminate in a Madame Hardy rather than a Dolly Parton" (113–14). Yet why—assuming we are to take this seriously—is one rose better than another, particularly when Pollan's gardener is given an aesthetic carte blanche? Disease resistance may play a role, but Pollan is otherwise disinterested in whether plants can survive without human assistance. We are left, then, to wonder how we judge whether a particular biological creation is worthy or "regrettable." A personal sense of beauty, it seems, is the only plausible guide. Yet if so, couldn't a gardener just as readily prefer the Dolly Parton (or a convenient compost pile over a useless statue)? Is the difference here one of personal taste alone, perhaps akin to the choice between Mendelssohn and the Grand Ole Opry?

A central weakness in all of this comes from the fact that in his critique of contemporary thought about humans in nature, Pollan has set his ideological poles too far apart. His portrait of nature domination is so extreme and his picture of the radical environmentalist so miscast (though both contain elements of truth) that just about everyone fits somewhere in between. Virtually the entire conservation movement does; so, too, do leaders of the American Farm Bureau Federation and leaders of the nation's big timber and pulp companies. Indeed, the most industrial of grain farmers or tree growers could easily read Pollan's narrative and nod in agreement, for as they see it they, too, are in the garden-tending business. They, too, work with nature, planting their chosen species, excluding weeds, and wooing nature to produce as much as possible. Pollan tells us to avoid the extremes but leaves us free to define the extremes as we see fit and then to wander unguided within the vast middle gulf.

In the end, Pollan's approach is merely a kinder, gentler form of land domination, and for that we can be grateful. But it is kinder and gentler not because these are inevitable parts of his garden image but because Pollan himself is kinder and gentler and because he hopes other gardeners will be, too. Pollan's ethical precept is simply too vague to provide guidance. It is too disconnected from the land, too lacking in any ecological base or any vision of a healthy land, too disconnected from the community, from other life, and from future generations. Then there is the intellectual isolation of it all: Pollan's unwillingness to engage (or even acknowledge) the vast bodies of serious writing on the subjects that he addresses: science, environmental ethics, environmental history (including histories of the environmental movement and environmental thought), environmental policy, and the deep cultural criticisms offered by David Ehrenfeld, David Orr, and other serious conservation writers.[13] His readers get the cartoon version.

We might highlight the many differences between Leopold and Pollan by placing side by side Leopold's community-minded farmer of the future, standing proud on his biologically diverse farm, and Pollan's gardener, surrounded by his high hedge and struggling daily to ward off his plant and animal "pests."

- Leopold's farmer manipulates his land and makes it grow, just like Pollan's gardener, but his farm is more than that and other than that. His thinking is ecological and linked to a vision of overall health.

Pollan's gardener, in contrast, ignores ecology and ecological interconnections. His vision ends at his garden's edge. For him, health is an attribute of individual organisms, not of the land community.

- For Leopold's farmer, beauty is linked to the healthy, the natural, and the appropriate. For Pollan's gardener, beauty is a personal choice, minimally constrained by nature or locale.
- Leopold's farmer is a member of a social community and feels obligated to sustain that community. Pollan's gardener is a loner, asking no help and offering none.
- Leopold's farmer loves the local wilds. Pollan's gardener loves the tame and pokes fun at naturalists.
- Leopold's farmer is proud of his farm's lengthy bird list. Pollan's gardener is proud of his many hues of well-tended roses.
- Leopold's farmer seeks to make room for wildlife. Pollan's gardener largely drives them out.
- Leopold's farmer surrounds his working fields with plants that are local and native. Pollan's gardener happily turns to the exotic.
- Leopold's farmer embraces an ethical orientation, undergirded by ecology and by an attentiveness to the enduring well-being of the surrounding community. Pollan's gardener embraces, as his ethical orientation, only a vague sense of self-restraint.

Armed with such a comparative list, one might

wonder about the popularity of Pollan's book and the garden thinking that it presents. Certainly the book's favorable reception suggests that the conservation cause needs to work harder, and better, in drawing attention to the root causes of degradation. Tend-the-garden reasoning implies that our conservation problems are easy ones, but they are not. They are difficult indeed, problems that challenge culture in profound ways.

Since Pollan's book appeared a decade ago, garden reasoning has mingled with other, similar strands of conservation thought, based on vague notions of stewardship, sustainability, and mild forms of "wise-use" thinking. More prevalent also has been the claim that conservation can happen if enough people simply develop fond feelings toward nature, or if they conjure up nostalgic memories of enjoying nature as children. Driven by such a love, they'll know what to do, just like Pollan's gardener. (Pollan's own work, it might be noted, has become more distinctly ecological and valuable, while retaining his enviable literary flair.)[14]

Those who embrace such ideas perhaps believe that they've recognized our environmental predicament and know how to solve it. Yet the ideas they offer, far from being new, are merely forms of the same cultural misdirections that have brought society to where it now is. We see a resurgence of human arrogance, so creative in many areas of human endeavor yet so destructive in others. We humans know enough to manipulate the land at will—so we tell ourselves and so we often believe. We can charge ahead, getting what we want, without thinking much about ecology; we can use self-created standards of beauty that are disconnected from any visions of enduring health.

Tend-the-garden thinking would have us shift back to a fragmented view of nature and to an atomistic understanding of the human experience, when it has been known for years that these attitudes have helped hurry the land's ecological decline. Individual landowners acting alone, this reasoning seems to say, can adequately deal with environmental problems, but the falsity of that position is or ought to be abundantly clear. From Leopold's rigorous land ethic we have in fact drifted to a watered-down, unscientific, easily manipulated ethic of simply being nice.

By avoiding the need for major cultural change, garden reasoning of this type overlaps with today's probusiness, libertarian calls for privatization and for unleashing the market. All such thinking resists the notion that America's individualistic, consumer-oriented culture is materially flawed. All of it rejects the worry, and the evidence, that human arrogance is much too vast.

Garden thinking provides a knotty challenge for serious conservationists convinced that the conservation cause can succeed only when science plays a key role and only when planning is done at landscape scales. By endorsing neither idea—and, indeed, by ignoring ecology entirely—garden reasoning is cause for dismay. The proper response to it, it would seem, is for conservationists to present their own serious views more clearly and forcefully. *Of course* we need to steer clear of the misanthropic ideas that Pollan rightfully condemns. Just as much, however, we need to distance ourselves from the kind of diluted, play-nice-with-nature sentiment that now enjoys such favor. Good science and clear, critical thought—taking conservation ideas seriously—are the precious currency of the day.

CHAPTER 4

Back to Sustainability

To the extent that there is an overall goal today for land conservation (defining *land* broadly, as before), it is likely to be, most people would say, *sustainability* or some similar term that includes the adjective *sustainable*. Other contenders for this role do exist, to be sure. For years, pockets of academics have pushed for a goal better grounded in science or nature, such as ecological integrity, biological diversity, or ecosystem health. Among the more radical activists, the call has gone out to restore our native fauna, particularly big predators, and to have that restoration serve as the conservation centerpiece. Then there is the more recent proposal that we turn to the new science of ecological restoration and use it both as a model of good land use and as a community-based activity that brings local people together to celebrate, explore, and nourish their home landscapes. These several contenders, though, have made only modest headway so far, important though they are. It is sustainability and its variants that dominate discussions, particularly in the halls of government and international finance.[1]

As anyone who has thought about the term knows, sustainability is characterized by an exceptional vagueness in that it leaves unstated the thing that is being sustained.[2] This vagueness is an obvious deficiency from the perspective of conservation advocates. Because it lacks clarity, sustainability is subject to a nearly infinite number of definitional variations, which undercuts the term's ability to provide meaningful guidance. This same vagueness, however, can also appear as a positive virtue, as some observers have noted.[3] For the diplomatically minded conference organizer, anxious to find consensus among varied constituencies, sustainability can provide an appealing middle policy ground where people with diverse views can meet. Individual proponents of sustainability might endorse conflicting ideas about what the term means, but at least they have agreed on something, and to agree on something is to begin down a path that could broaden.[4]

The popularity of sustainability raises obvious questions for serious conservationists. How should we think about the term, and what should we do with it? Might sustainability have value despite its vagueness, particularly if the vagueness can somehow lessen over time? Or do we need to view it with greater suspicion, perhaps as a Trojan horse that we've unwisely allowed into our midst?

The noun sustainability is apparently new to the English language, first appearing in dictionaries in the late 1980s. The word's roots are the thirteenth-century French *sustenir* and the Latin *sustinere,* meaning to hold up or support something from below. As a verb, to sustain originally served to connect a subject that was doing the sustaining to the object that was being sustained. In the land-use arena, the root idea of sustaining, at least when used in the sense of intensive scientific management for economic efficiency, first gained visibility two centuries ago in the sustained-yield forestry programs of Germany, according to historian Donald Worster.[5] From there it drifted across the Atlantic in the late nineteenth century, in part through the efforts of Gifford Pinchot and other Americans who studied German forestry methods and were eager to try them here. During the Progressive Era, the ideal of sustained yield was applied to other natural resources and even to entire river systems, which were viewed as having multiple values when managed scientifically.[6]

In the 1970s the adjective sustainable came to describe a new orientation toward farming. Wes Jackson was perhaps the first to propose a sustainable agriculture, though the core idea had long been known.[7] (In the United States, according to historian Steven Stoll, an important conservation effort early in the nineteenth century had something like sustainable agriculture as its aim.)[8] Wes Jackson offered his new vision as an alternative to the industrial approach to agriculture, which Wendell Berry had so forcefully attacked around the same time in his important book *The Unsettling of America*.[9]

Used as an adjective to modify development, sustainable first appeared (again according to Worster) in the *World Conservation Strategy*, issued in 1980 by the International Union for the Conservation of Nature. The term obviously struck a responsive chord, for it quickly began appearing elsewhere. Lester R. Brown of the Worldwatch Institute gave it prominence in one of his books. From there the term's rise continued until it gained its most enduring application in *Our Common Future* (1987), the report of the World Commission on Environment and Development directed by Norwegian prime minister Gro Harlem Brundtland.[10] As defined in the Brundtland Report, sustainable development meant "development that meets the needs of the present without compromising the ability of future generations to meet their own needs."[11]

Sustainable development proved particularly attractive in the international arena as a means of urging both developed and less-developed countries to agree in broad principle on resource-use policies. The sustainability part of the term acknowledged nature's limits and encouraged countries to live within them. The development part showed awareness of global poverty and of the need for poor countries to ratchet up their levels of production and consumption. In the years since the Brundtland Report, *sustainable* as adjective has been used to modify an almost countless number of nouns. Thus, we now have "sustainable societies," "sustainable institutions," "sustainable planet," "sustainable future," and so on (including, from the U.S. Department of Agriculture, "making a sustainable difference").[12]

Hardly had the banner of sustainability been unfurled when observers began pointing to its suspect malleability. Even when used to modify a specific noun, such as agriculture, sustainable seemed to be long on aspiration and short on solid meaning. In the farm setting in particular the term quickly gained a variety of meanings. In Wes Jackson's view, industrial agriculture was manifestly unsustainable in that it depended on finite stocks of fossil fuel energy and sapped the soil of its natural fertility.[13] Jackson, though, had no copyright on the term. In the hands of others more friendly to agribusiness, the term soon meant agriculture that kept farmers and rural communities afloat, or agriculture that maintained particular dominant crops, or even public policies that upheld industrial agriculture and the profits of agribusiness companies.

In a thorough study published in 1994, agriculture scientist Greg McIsaac attempted to bring order to this definitional chaos. His conclusion, to no surprise, was that variations in meanings were fueled by conflicts of fundamental social values and intellectual paradigms, which the term *sustainable agriculture* merely papered over.[14] In a report published at about the same time, two rural sociologists reached similar conclusions. Their bottom line: the normative literature on natural resource sustainability divided itself into no fewer than nine distinct categories, so widely varied as to yield little common ground.[15]

Alongside this problem of *what* we are supposed to sustain, though attracting less attention, has been the uncertainty about *who* or what is doing the sustaining. When sustainable modifies a human-activity noun, such as agriculture, it would seem that people are the ones doing the work. Agriculture is a human enterprise, with humans calling the shots. Plainly, a danger lurks in this arrangement for serious conservationists. When humans do the sustaining, we set ourselves up as operators if not masters of nature's systems. Such terms suggest, if they do not overtly proclaim, that humans are the subjects, nature is the object, and the human task and privilege is to manipulate the land however we like. There is truth to this claim, of course, as a matter of raw control; we do influence nature and have no choice but to do so. But conservationists would like to hear, in the same first utterance, a clear recognition that human powers are limited and that we would do well, when using the land, to study and respect nature's embedded ways.

The reason we have environmental problems is not because there is something wrong with our planet. It is because we are not living well on it, which is to say our behavior toward nature is somehow deficient. Our behavior patterns, in turn, are linked to human arrogance and to our exceptional faith in reason (among many other factors), which means we need to act more humbly and respectfully. These are basic conservation truths. And they are truths easily forgotten when humans are assigned the task of "sustaining" nature.

When sustainable is attached to a noun such as planet or future, the human actor disappears. We are then at a loss to know who or what is doing the sustaining. Nature itself, perhaps? The Creator? No doubt the Earth will continue in its orbit pretty much without regard to what happens to humans. And as for the future, it will come upon us no matter what we do, short of inventing some time-stopping mechanism. Who, then, is sustaining what?

Presumably, terms such as sustainable planet and sustainable future are meant to impose constraints upon the ways we live on the planet to improve our descendants' lives. But what kinds of behavioral limits and to what end? Is the implication here that the planet's biosphere and our planetary future ought to be shaped predominantly by nonhuman forces? If that's the intended implication, can we not find a way to say so more clearly?

Confusing matters even more is the fact that sustainability is used variously both as a means and as an end. The *means* we employ are presumably sustainable if we can repeat them over and over. But how do we apply this test to the aspects of nature that are nonrenewable (fossil fuel deposits, for instance)? Should we leave them entirely alone? And what about the fact that the living, renewable parts of nature are evolving and would do so even without human intervention? How do we sustain something that is inherently dynamic? The key point here: to focus merely on the sustainability of *means* is to leave entirely open the kind of lives we want to live and the kind of natural surroundings we want to enjoy.

When used as an *end*, sustainability is literally incoherent—it has no meaning—until it is matched with a noun, implicitly or explicitly. There must be some *thing* that is being sustained. But which noun are we to use? An obvious choice would be some component of nature, such as biological diversity or overall primary productivity. By why choose one natural component over another? And indeed, why choose a component of nature as opposed to some human activity? Standing alone, the term sustainability gives no clue of what we ought to sustain.

As defined in *Our Common Future*, sustainable development looks not at nature (or not directly at least) but instead at the satisfaction of human needs and aspirations. "Overriding priority" is given to the satisfaction today of the essential needs of the world's poor; all else, apparently, comes later, in the event these fundamental human needs are ever met.[16] Although sustainable development, we are told, does include "the idea of limitations," its built-in limits apparently arise out of our "technology and social organization" rather than from any enduring constraints imposed by nature.[17] Because our technology and organizations are themselves subject to change (and indeed we are supposed to be busily changing them to achieve this goal), sustainable development when defined this way could impose little or even no long-term constraints on how we live.[18] We can achieve sustainable development, the Brundtland Report seems to tell us, merely by tinkering with our technology and by crafting better organizational arrangements. There is no need, apparently, for us to change ourselves; there is no need to diminish our arrogance or to alter our ways of perceiving and valuing nature.

As the Brundtland Report illustrates, the idea of sustainability need not be linked directly to nature or to nature's functioning. It need not, therefore, make any use of the science of ecology nor emphasize to a distracted world that humans are embedded in and dependent on the larger systems of nature. Along with this inattention (directly at least) to science and nature, there is a corresponding lack of any clear link to morality and to the idea of ethical constraints. Ethics could easily play a role in sustainability; in many definitions, of course, it does. But sustainability standing alone supplies precious little moral guidance. If it is to have a moral content, that content needs to be injected from the outside.

This inattention to ethics is surprising, because if sustainability means anything on its own, it is for us "to consider the long term," which is to say to consider future generations. To mention future generations is to imply that we have an ethical duty of some sort that relates to them. It is to propose, one would reasonably assume, that our dealings with nature ought to take into account the welfare of our descendants. Yet, if that is the message implicit in sustainability, then we ought to be asking ourselves more deliberately: Why is this the case? Why should we be worrying about future generations? If we had an answer to that question, it might shed light on what sustainability really means.

Several moral theories can be rounded up to help our thinking about future generations. It could be (as some philosophers urge) that future generations enter our moral scheme indirectly, as the beneficiaries of a duty on our part to respect nature's intrinsic value. It could be instead that concern for the future is an attribute of being virtuous today; it is a way to implement the age-old adage "If you make a mess, clean it up" or perhaps some variant of "When staying in a hotel, don't steal the towels." A more direct way to respect future generations is to assert that they have their own moral value, which we are duty bound to respect. Whatever our line of reasoning, we might gain much-needed guidance if we pursued the reasoning soberly. And yet, sustainability advocates seem to have little interest in this challenging intellectual chore.[19]

Conservationists, in sum, find quite a list of reasons to look askance at sustainability: its vagueness and confusion, its troublesome policy implications, its detachment from nature and morality, its deceptive appearance of consensus and forward motion. Along with these, and no less important, is a rather practical deficiency: sustainability is uninspired and uninspiring. It is just plain dull.

Sustainability for many implies a life that is stagnant and repetitive. It implies restrictions that keep us from growing, changing, and enjoying new experiences. Bureaucrats might find the term useful, given its all-things-to-all-people flexibility. But politicians are well aware of its rhetorical limpness. Voters like candidates who talk about a better future, not about staying in a rut. Even former vice president Al Gore, so committed to conservation, came to see that sustainability had no political traction.[20] It drew little public attention, much less voter excitement. As an inspiration, sustainability ranks low indeed.

For many people, the central insight of sustainability is that we ought to consume nature's resources at rates and in ways that we will be able to continue. For some, this means cutting back on current levels of use. For others, it means maintaining or elevating consumption levels by manipulating nature more efficiently than we have in the past. But whether consumption rates are supposed to go up or down, the core idea is the same: we should consume nature at rates that can endure.[21]

This is a familiar view of nature, of course—nature perceived in fragmented terms, with some parts valuable and others not. We have seen it before. Value here is determined by reference to human needs, whether basic or extravagant. Humans, by implication, are the sole holders of moral value, and nature exists merely as a backdrop and as a resource warehouse. So long as we're prudent and scientific in our dealings with nature, we can manipulate it as aggressively as we like.

These ideas are familiar not only because they dominate resource discussions today but because of their venerable historical pedigree. The ideas are lifted, nearly verbatim, from the conservation philosophy of Gifford Pinchot and colleagues during the administration of President Theodore Roosevelt.[22]

Pinchot's conservation message a century ago was clear and widely appealing. People could have it all, he predicted, if they would only use sound science and economics to manage the land—which is to say if they would only defer on resource-use issues to the trained experts. Conservation meant full resource use. To conserve a river's flow in arid country meant to use water so completely that not a drop reached the sea.[23] To conserve a forest was to manage it for maximum sustained yield while protecting adjacent, human-used water flows. Pinchot had little to say about nature's limits or about the wisdom of respecting its time-crafted ways, except as needed to keep valuable resources flowing abundantly. Nature itself had no intrinsic value, and people could ignore the parts of nature not linked to human utility. As for the moral side of resource use, that issue arose only when resources were overtly wasted, or when one person hoarded so many resources that other people had no reasonable access to them.[24]

So far as one can tell, sustainability as commonly defined today overlaps considerably with this conservation wisdom from a century ago. Pinchot's ideas, in turn, drew upon the thought and work of a slightly earlier generation of American conservationists. Elite easterners for the most part, they lamented the declines of game species and sought to protect them by limiting hunting levels to sustainable yields. Wild animals existed largely to shoot or to watch.

Conservation was about keeping them around for that purpose.[25]

In sustainability, then, what we have is an idea that largely dates from the late nineteenth century, the dawning age of organized national conservation. To propose at this point that we embrace sustainability for the twenty-first century is thus to pose an obvious question: Have we learned nothing important about land conservation in the intervening century? Did these early conservationists get things right, intellectually speaking, so that we need merely to follow their good lead? Or, instead, has conservation thought gained in wisdom since then, so that we would be remiss in turning back the clock?

The answer, of course, is that we have learned things, a great deal in fact. We can begin cataloguing this hard-earned wisdom by noting the difficulties that arise when we try to implement Pinchot's sustained-yield ideal. Management for sustained yield, it turns out, is far harder on the ground than Pinchot's era realized. Maximum yields and carrying capacities are difficult to calculate and subject to unexpected change. As fisheries biologist P. A. Larkin has concluded, "No one can deny that hypothetical animal populations can produce hypothetical maximum sustained yields, but the same cannot be said of any real animal populations that are really being harvested."[26] Conspicuous among our sustained-yield failures has been our inability to manage fisheries without depleting breeding stocks.

Also conspicuous, in light of Pinchot's personal expertise in forestry, has been our continued use of tree-growing practices that inexorably deplete natural fertility. Ever-greater chemical inputs are required to keep timber production levels from falling. Real environments, it turns out, are complex, interconnected, and dynamic, more so than Pinchot and his colleagues understood. A sustained-yield formula is not adequate to distinguish land use from land abuse. That is lesson number one.

We have also come to see the limitations in Pinchot's multiple-use ideal. To manage land to increase harvests of one or a few species, whether of elk, lobsters, or loblolly pine, is to diminish the land's value for other wild species. Game managers in the 1930s learned this lesson when they saw how high populations of one desired species (deer, most visibly) could degrade the habitat for other species.[27] John von Neumann and Oskar Morgenstern gave this field observation a mathematical grounding in 1947. In an interlinked system, they showed, it is possible to maximize only one variable at a time.[28] As biologist-philosopher David Ehrenfeld put it, we cannot make everything "best" simultaneously.[29] Choices have to be made, and it is good to make them wisely: lesson number two.

Progressive Era conservationists managed land to produce the particular resources that fetched good market prices. They were prepared, for instance, to build reservoirs for power and irrigation without concern for plummeting fish populations—for them the less important resource.[30] Within two decades, their more ecologically minded successors (beginning in the 1920s) would challenge this wisdom, at least when applied broadly. Aldo Leopold perhaps went the furthest right before World War II. Conservation, Leopold claimed, should not be about augmenting particular flows of resources. It should be about keeping the entire land community healthy and functioning; if that were done, humans could enjoy a diverse, naturally integrated set of resource flows.[31] Narrowly focused land management made sense when nature seemed to possess only a few valuable parts. A much different management ideal was needed when nature's values were understood more broadly.

Conflicts over managing land for multiple uses became more obvious in the 1920s, as resource managers added to the list of resource uses compiled in the Progressive Era. With each new resource use came increased competition among the resources, particularly on federal lands. Wildlife advocates pressed to protect the many species that were enjoyable to look at, not just the few species that people could shoot or hook.[32] To do that, though, land-use changes had to take place. Ecologists, led by Victor Shelford of Illinois, called for the identification and preservation of unaltered natural areas, particularly high-quality examples for scientists to study.[33] Again, the proposal created land-use conflicts. As roads crisscrossed the country, reaching deep into federal enclaves, advocates of wilderness recreation clamored for protecting big roadless areas.[34] Their call was seconded by the increasingly vocal conservationists concerned about the plight of rare species, big predators included. On the East Coast, Benton MacKaye pushed for the creation of the Appalachian Trail and other recreational corridors—so vital, he claimed, to the human spirit.[35] MacKaye's particular worry was about the highways that were altering the landscape, spreading cities outward and separating urban residents even further from direct contact with nature.[36]

Step by step, the list of resource uses was becoming more numerous. Not all resource values could be satisfied in a given place. When it came to managing land, that is, we could not have it all. Lesson three: When a landscape had many valuable parts, not just a few, the sustained-yield model collapsed. It was not possible to sustain maximum yields of everything, and sustained yield as an idea gave no guidance on how to make trade-offs.

What conservationists of the interwar period could see, better than their Progressive Era predecessors, was how the land's ecological interconnection posed grave challenges for land management. The science of manipulating land became more complex, particularly as people perceived and evaluated land in new ways. Year by year, scientists compiled evidence of the land's interdependence. Year by year, it became more evident that action in one place sent ripples throughout the ecological whole.[37] When humans and their aspirations were added to the picture, the conservation challenge became even harder. Humans needed frequent contact with nature if they were to thrive, physically and mentally. To relegate wild nature to distant locations, away from cities, was to cut people off from nature's healing power. Hadn't America's character been forged on the frontier? Hadn't democracy arisen and gained strength from the availability of open spaces and opportunities? Lesson four: Because nature was linked to our spirits and souls as a people, it was not enough to manage land simply to fill our stomachs.

Then there was the harsh reality of resource misuse, made so apparent by the Dust Bowl. This land-use catastrophe was not caused by nature, as sensitive observers at the time could plainly see. Droughts and winds were long-standing natural aspects of semiarid places. The true causes of failure lay in our radical individualism, our commitment to a laissez-faire version of private property, and our belief that technology could overcome any challenges that nature posed. Empowered by the law of property, driven by the market, and unchecked by any ecological understanding, western farmers plowed land that should have been left in grass.[38] In doing so, they mimicked their predecessors in Kentucky, the Carolina Piedmont, and so many other places who had plowed hillsides prone to quick erosion.[39] Topsoil was an ecologically vital resource, and we had squandered it for generations. It was valuable and deserved protection, according to Hugh Hammond Bennett and others in the 1930s, even though it brought no cash on the market.[40] Lesson five: land misuse was embedded in American culture and its core institutions, private property in particular, which meant that America could conserve only by undergoing significant cultural change.

The Dust Bowl and other land-use problems, many of them in the South, encouraged conservationists of the 1930s and 1940s to ask bigger questions about how Americans were inhabiting and using the continent. Economist Lewis C. Gray, the Agriculture Department's land-utilization visionary, talked openly about practicing conservation on a continental scale. In ways that echoed and augmented John Wesley Powell's arguments from the previous century, Gray called for regional or even national land planning to achieve a wide array of goals: ecological, social, and economic.[41] A similar call arose from Lewis Mumford, whose concerns gave particular emphasis to aesthetics, morals, and the conveniences of human life.[42] Aldo Leopold may have been the most ecologically guided conservation writer of the day, but in his proposal for a new orientation toward land and land use, an orientation quite different from Pinchot's, Leopold was joined by others. What was needed (lesson six) was a conservation vision that extended to entire landscapes and that included working lands, working people, and the full array of human needs and desires.

Two factors, perhaps more than others, were animating this ongoing growth of serious conservation thought: an increasing attention to ecological interconnection and a growing recognition of nature's inherent, inscrutable complexity. Nature, it was being discovered, was more dynamic, more interwoven, and more unfathomable than people had realized. In its intricacy it could get out of order and thus fail to meet human needs, without regard to whether humans were overharvesting its usable parts. To keep the land functioning we needed to recognize our ignorance and act more humbly. We needed to make use of our intuition—that slowly developed skill talked about by Leopold—rather than rely strictly on empirical data and the findings of science. Technology, in fact, often caused as many problems as it solved. Human reason was less potent than people presumed. For some observers, this was the glue that kept all of the other lessons together.

The lessons learned by lead conservationists between 1920 and 1950 were by no means embraced by everyone—far from it. Indeed, the later lessons on the list were learned by only a few, at least as solid conclusions that became new building blocks. In terms of practical implementation, little was accomplished even when thoughtful conservationists such as Lewis

Gray and Rex Tugwell guided the land-use policies of Roosevelt's New Deal. Still, the wisdom of the ages as seen by conservation's intellects was put down on paper for later generations to consider. Their visionary ideas lingered, and post–World War II conservationists would build on some of them. William Vogt echoed many of Aldo Leopold's ideas in his best-selling book from 1948, *Road to Survival.*[43] Postwar ecologists further clarified understandings of nutrient and energy flows as they studied trophic levels and the land's productivity. By then, predators were being respected for their roles in supporting healthy lands.[44] The call to preserve all life forms and representative wild areas had become loud indeed. Moreover, it was by then clear, or nearly so, that human needs were sometimes met best by leaving nature alone rather than engineering it—by allowing its floodplains to control flooding, for instance, and its wetlands to cleanse polluted water.

By late in the century, in sum, much had changed in the conservation world. Leading conservation scientists were struggling to bring it all together into a new paradigm to replace Pinchot's sustained-yield, multiple-use perspective. Biological diversity, ecological integrity, ecosystem health—these and similar terms were crafted as tools to talk about a more holistic, ecologically based conservation policy.[45] Making the search for a new paradigm all the harder was the bountiful evidence of nature's inherent dynamism.

Scientists had long known that nature changed but had never successfully translated that knowledge into land-use principles.[46] Inevitably, as this scientific work continued apace, individual conservationists tried to convert leading biological ideas into economic language, to take advantage of the widespread popularity of economic jargon. Some of them began speaking of the "ecosystem services" that nature provided, others about "natural capitalism."[47] Also popular at century's end was the idea of the "ecological footprint," a notion that directly connected global ecological decline to the life choices and consumptive practices of individuals.[48]

Taking place at the same time as these scientific advances was a fertile conversation about the moral implications of our place in the natural order. The terminology and modes of analysis here were, if anything, even more varied than those developed by competing scientists. Yet, by standing back from the details it was nonetheless possible to see a clear shift away from the conservation precepts of a century ago. The moral universe was not nearly so divided between morally worthy humans and morally empty nature. Indeed, the mere idea that humans could be thought about and valued apart from nature made less and less ecological sense. Science had irretrievably embedded humans into a complex, dynamic, interdependent natural order. It became the task of philosophers, then, to work out the implications of this embeddedness.[49]

By the beginning of the twenty-first century, conservation thought had progressed far indeed from the century before. So vast have the changes been that it is hard to catalogue and summarize them all. Details aside, though, the chief conclusion ought to be clear: conservation today is not—it simply cannot be—the sustained-yield thought of a century ago dressed up in the newer garb of sustainable development, sustainable planet, or sustainability. To view it that way would be to turn our backs on the wisdom that our conservation predecessors (including many still at work) have labored so hard to gain.

Pinchot's view of conservation made the work of conservation far too easy. He focused on just a few resources, he radically underestimated nature's complexity, and he challenged only modestly the cultural roots of our land-degrading behaviors. The path he proposed was, in retrospect, wide and easy. It is little wonder, then, that so many people today look back to it with fondness. To go back to conservation Pinchot-style is to brush aside so many of today's nagging challenges. Why confront the serious components of today's conservation thought when we can rally around the simpler ideas of generations ago? When the wide, easy road is so appealing as common ground, why keep talking about the narrow, arduous way? Can't we just view nature as a garden that we can tend sensitively? Can't we just develop sustainable ways of living or find some easy, gold-bricked road to a sustainable future?[50]

As a conservation goal, sustainability would hardly seem worth considering, so grave and numerous are its deficiencies. What makes the term worth a closer look is the fact that it is often defined as much more than just a conservation aim. The term has become, for many, an all-purpose vision of how humans ought to live in relation to nature and one another. Sustainability is meant to be, that is, a term that integrates conservation issues with various social and economic concerns to produce an overarching target for planetwide reform efforts.[51]

It is worth noting, as a first step in assessing this broader definition of sustainability, that the conservation cause has long embraced human needs and social justice. Conservation has kept a rather clear focus on land and land use, broadly defined, but the motive driving this work has mostly been to help people over the long term. Progressive Era conservationists expressly promoted waterway projects to increase the direct benefits people got from their rivers and to make more irrigated land available in small parcels for poor families.[52] Lewis Gray's work in the 1930s was similarly driven by express concerns that families were being pushed onto ecologically marginal lands that could not sustain them very long.[53] Aldo Leopold, the first prominent advocate for wilderness preservation, was worried initially and foremost about the decline of roadless areas where people could go to engage in a particularly American form of outdoor recreation.[54]

Again and again, conservationists talked about the ways conservative land use made human life better.

What divided conservationists from their business-friendly opponents was thus not a nature versus humanity conflict. The dividing line was different and more complex. Conservation's opponents favored short-term exploitive profits; conservationists (by mid- to late century) talked about long-term health and welfare. Opponents saw most land as producing a single commodity; conservationists looked to a wide suite of human benefits, some valued in the market, others not. Opponents viewed land as a mechanism to tinker with however they liked and to discard once exhausted; conservationists saw it as a complex, interdependent web of life that we ought to inhabit in perpetuity.

From the side of conservation's opponents, predictably, this dividing line has appeared in a much different light. Conservation is costly, so its opponents have claimed. It interferes with economic opportunities, thus frustrating human aspirations. But hard evidence lends little support to these familiar criticisms, at least when long-term concerns are given due weight. Conservation measures, to be sure, can harm the individual landowner or business by denying opportunities for profit. Conservation measures can also terminate real jobs. But when economic calculations are broadened to include all factors and the long term—when they consider neighbors, the surrounding community, and distant places as well as the individual landowner or jobholder—conservation typically makes good sense.[55] Job losses in one place are often offset by gains elsewhere. Conservation often involves substantial costs saving.

Given these considerations—particularly those relating to alleged costs and to conservation's long-standing concern about human welfare—there is ample reason to worry about sustainability when the term is defined so as to encompass a variety of social justice considerations not involving direct human-nature interactions. The rhetoric about sustainability as a catchall aspiration, including social justice along with land-use issues, appears to concede that conservation's critics are basically right. It presumes that conservation stands in tension with economic growth and social justice, with trade-offs therefore necessary. Sustainability then becomes one grand umbrella covering a variety of competing concerns. Under that umbrella compromises are made, and the ultimate outcome is a package of policies that promotes sustainability writ large. Thus, in an effort to promote sustainability, we can end up endorsing policies that are harsh on nature and that cannot be continued in any ecological sense. And yet, the policies are said to promote sustainability because of their social justice implications.

As noted, hard evidence supporting the need for such trade-offs is really rather scarce, at least when we embrace something more than a short-term, localized perspective and are willing to consider significant changes in existing ways of doing business. Evidence about conflict (and thus the need for compromise) typically comes in anecdotal form, as stories about the harsh effects that regulations have on an individual land parcel or on an individual jobholder or business. When an identifiable individual or local area suffers economically, the cries of unfairness and high cost arise. But again, there is the bigger picture to consider. The job losses in one place are recorded, the job gains elsewhere too often overlooked. We forget that a development project banned from one place can often go elsewhere. A well-planned community, laced with greenways and compactly settled, can improve human life and elevate land values, compared with a community that arises haphazardly.

Conservationists need to be cautious, then, when sustainability advocates propose to add conservation issues into a larger mix of social goals. Just such an offer is implicit in the proposal to define sustainability as a mixture of economics, environment, and equity (the three E's, they are sometimes termed). It is possible, of course, to promote conservation in ways that undercut economic needs and that aggravate inequities. It is sensible, accordingly, to remind ourselves that these cultural elements are also important. But when the three E's are merely listed, the implication is inevitable: environment comes at a cost to equity and economics.

How, then, should conservationists consider sustainability when it is defined in such a socially inclusive manner? One problem with this approach is that sustainability then becomes, if possible, even more vague than before. A graver practical problem is that conservationists swept into sustainability writ large are left with no way to talk about their own specific aims and no way to measure progress in achieving them. Indeed, with sustainability so all encompassing, it becomes hard to say with assurance that any land-use condition conflicts with sustainability.

So long as conservationists have an ecological goal tied to the land's functioning, they can point to eroding topsoil as a clear failure. But what happens when we add equity and economics to the picture and the erosion is being caused by a small farm family on the brink of poverty? Or what happens when the erosion comes from a development project that brings jobs and economic growth? Despite the erosion, the overall project might seem to promote sustainability rather than diminish it. Or so one could argue. Our practices can become more sustainable—even as the land slides down!

The point is that when sustainability is defined so inclusively, conservation interests are at grave risk of getting lost in the shuffle. The game becomes one of trade-offs, and to enter the game is to consent to the bargaining process. Conservationists can vigorously challenge any concessions, of course; they can deny the conflicts and argue forcefully for their concerns. But the argument turns into one about details. Without a separate goal, conservationists have no good way to measure where things stand, vis-à-vis the land. Without separate rhetoric, it is hard to heighten the public's awareness of ecological considerations. It is hard to draw attention to the ethical and aesthetic considerations that serious conservation includes.

Within the United States there is little reason why the basic ecological and ethical aims of conservation need to be traded off against economic and equity considerations. Our farms produce more food than we need. So why do we degrade waterways with irrigation and polluted runoff, growing an overabundance of crops? Why do we allow excessive grazing in semiarid landscapes to produce beef that is easily produced elsewhere with far less harm? Why do we permit sheep raisers to kill wolves in the few places where wolves live, when wool is nearly worthless and when mutton is easily raised in places without wolf conflicts? Wetland drainage efforts (to cite another example) are notorious for bringing net overall costs. Farm subsidies go to encourage corn growing on sloping lands that lose soil, even as we scurry around trying to find markets where we can dump our excess crops. When the new Wal-Mart is blocked to preserve open space, the cry goes up about job losses, as if we did not know full well, from study after study, that the coming of Wal-Mart costs jobs and tends to lower local pay scales.[56]

A particularly good example of how conservation can bring widespread benefits rather than costs is provided by beef production today, which features huge feedlots. Cattle are fed subsidized corn, they generate wastes that are a serious pollution problem, and they are injected with pharmaceuticals to promote growth and ward off disease. Meanwhile, eroding soils are pressed into service to provide the corn, leading to lost soil fertility, the siltation of waterways, chemical runoff into rivers, unnaturally fast drainage (which exacerbates flooding and drought), and tilled fields that are almost worthless as wildlife habitat. All the while, the corn production consumes large quantities of fossil fuels, purchased with tax exemptions, leading to air and atmospheric degradation. An alternative, of course, has long been known (other than to cut back on beef consumption): put cattle back in pastures, have them eat grass, and stop tilling the land (thus halting the erosion, the polluted runoff, and the altered drainage). Subsidies for the corn growing can be ended and fossil fuel usage (and hence air pollution) reduced. As wildlife habitat, pasture is far better than tilled fields, and cattle can be raised with few or no pharmaceuticals. Best of all, grass-fed meat is healthier to consume.[57]

An end to massive cattle feedlots, of course, is not soon to happen. Nor is Illinois (to choose one example) soon to get tough with agricultural water pollution, given the political clout of industrial agriculture. Farm subsidies are deployed to encourage higher yields of overproduced commodities, and hardly at all to foster conservation. These political decisions and similar ones could be challenged. They very much need to be challenged. But the challenges won't succeed unless and until the conservation cause speaks with clarity, coherence, and passion.

In the wealthy United States of today it is highly questionable to assert that conservation cannot be afforded, or that conservation stands in the way of helping the poor meet their basic needs. To grow the economic pie has long been the proposed solution to raising the living standards of the poor. Whatever merit the argument once had, it deserves little credit today, given how free trade and liberal immigration policies work to ensure that the lowest paying jobs stay low paying. A bigger pie seems unlikely to help much in the foreseeable future. America's problem is in the increasingly unequal way that pie is divided, which in turn is due to laws and deliberate public policies in addition to market forces.

In the political battles that take place daily, and in the arena of public rhetoric that supplies the context, sustainability is largely worthless for serious conservation advocates. The sooner we discard it the better.

CHAPTER 5

What Is Good Land Use?

I f conservation is to regain its bearings, the place to begin is with the land, broadly defined, and with the people living on and drawing sustenance from it. Conservation, ultimately, is about promoting good land uses for the benefit of people, future generations, and the land itself. But what is good land use? What are its characteristics or elements, and how do they fit together? Is the best way to identify good land use to start with the land and its ecological functioning and then add the people, tailoring their activities so as to sustain that functioning?

Or should we begin instead with the people and their needs and then insert nature into the mix?

The instinct of scientists is to begin with nature; that's the aspect they know best. The instinct of economists, typically, is to begin instead with the market and with the production and exchange of goods and services and then somehow adjust the market to take better care of nature. A third approach, popular among some conservationists, is to begin with the human-nature bond in emotional terms and to ask how we might persuade people to love nature more. Here the assumption is that if people really cared about nature in their hearts, all else would largely fall into place; a more specific, ecologically based goal is apparently unneeded.[1]

Then there are the many people who approach land-use issues in fragmented terms, one parcel at a time, rarely pausing to consider landscapes as a whole. This last approach, probably the most common one, has the considerable virtue of practicality. When a land-use problem is obvious, why not tackle the problem directly instead of viewing it as a small part of something much bigger? Tract-by-tract conservation work largely fits into this category. Preserve a piece here, buy an easement or development right there, and perhaps all will work for the best.

None of these approaches starts from what ought to be the obvious place. Inevitably, people are the ones who decide whether land use is good. The logical place to begin, then, is not with science or with nature, much less with the market or with a simple love of the wilds. It is with a direct question: What makes land use good for people?

This question, it turns out, is a fruitful one, because it is relatively easy to identify the broad factors to use in evaluating land uses. The factors fall into three basic categories. Once we identify and explore these, spreading all the factors on the table, we can appreciate the many building blocks of good land use. We are also better positioned to spot the omissions and deficiencies that afflict much of today's conservation rhetoric.[2]

Human utility, broadly defined. Embedded as they are in nature, people necessarily depend upon the land for daily sustenance. Good land use needs to meet these basic needs—for everyone, if possible. A good life, though, entails far more than just food, clothing, and shelter. There are the beauties that a surrounding landscape can provide, in terms of both the natural and the built environment. There are the conveniences and satisfactions that come when a home territory is well laid out and arranged in ways that foster healthy social interactions. Sometimes people want to escape society; good land use would offer remote places for them to go. Many people enjoy interacting with wild creatures, whether at backyard bird feeders or in secluded locations. Good land use would make this possible as well.

Once we start enumerating the many ways that good land use benefits people, the list turns out to be quite long. And it gets longer when we go beyond the immediate direct benefits and consider the types of land uses *indirectly* required if the land is to continue supplying these direct benefits. For soil to remain fertile and productive, for instance, soil fertility cycles need to keep functioning, which in turn has implications for the protection of biological diversity. For fisheries to remain productive, rivers and lakes also need to be healthy, which means water flows that are reasonably clean and not significantly altered in physical terms. Genetic diversity—a wide range of plants and animals—needs to be respected to ensure the continued viability of species that are directly and indirectly useful to people. Natural areas also require protection, not only because they directly benefit people but so that scientists can study them and gain the lessons needed to manage lands well. Then there are the many species and natural processes that play vital roles in keeping pests and diseases in check. Human utility, in short, is complexly tied to the land's biotic composition and ecological functioning, as ecologists over the past century have so often said.[3]

There is little need to be fully comprehensive here in listing the ways that good land use can benefit people, because the central conclusion is easily stated. *Good land use would promote overall human utility,* with utility defined broadly to include aesthetics and quality-of-life issues as well as bread-and-butter needs.

When utility is defined this way, it is clear that it extends beyond the particular resource uses that are assigned prices by the market. Many land-use benefits lack market prices, though they are highly valuable to people, because they are never bought and sold. The market deals only in commodities and services that people can purchase and consume personally, without significantly sharing benefits with others. Clean air, healthy rivers, abundant wildlife, fertility cycles, stratospheric ozone, well-functioning atmospheric processes, basic disturbance regimes: these and many other components of nature, essential to human utility, carry no market price. Many are "public goods" in the sense that the public as a whole benefits from them, without regard for who pays. The market, notoriously, undervalues such goods.[4] Other ecological benefits are more localized but still shared among enough people so that the person bearing the cost is unable to capture all the benefits. For this reason (along with others), it makes little sense to think that the market alone can dictate good land use, however useful it is in achieving more limited goals.

Human utility is no doubt the central factor defining good land use. For many people it is likely the only one. For the serious conservationist, though, other factors are also relevant; the bar of good land use is set higher.

Ethical considerations. Standing beside human utility is a constellation of factors that might be termed ethical. They, too, play significant roles in defining good land use. When people use ethical considerations in evaluating land-use behaviors, then the goodness of their land use will depend upon whether they have abided by these considerations. The point is a rather simple one, yet it is rarely mentioned directly and its implications are easy to overlook.[5]

Looming large in this second, ethics category is the whole matter of future generations. The popular goal of sustainability (as noted in chapter 4) presumes that people living today ought to look out for their descendants. Most people agree. What this duty entails, of course, is far from clear. But whatever shape the duty takes, it plays a vital role in defining good land use. Land use is good only when it fulfills the ethical obligations that people today have to tend the land for future generations.

This component, it needs emphasizing, could prove exceptionally influential if we decide to define broadly our obligations vis-à-vis the future. If we feel obligated to protect all life forms for future generations to enjoy (a widely held ideal), then land use will be good only when it achieves this conservation result. If our duties (instead or in addition) include the maintenance of representative examples of all types of natural areas, or perhaps the protection of the land's overall natural productive capacity, then land use again will be good only if these duties are fulfilled. Land use is not good when these duties are breached.

A duty to future generations makes sense only when understood as a *collective* duty of people now living. It is implausible to think of it merely as a duty imposed upon an individual as such, to fulfill or not as the individual sees fit. Practically speaking, no individual could remotely fulfill such a duty. Here again, we stumble upon a potent reason why we cannot rely entirely upon the market to foster good land use. The market leads to land uses that benefit people living today, the landowner above all. Although the market does permit landowners to use their lands in ways that respect the future, individual owners can often accomplish little acting alone. Which individual alone can save a species, or protect the Earth's soil, or halt the degradation of unique natural areas? Any sensible expression of a duty to future generations would require planning at large spatial scales. Only with such a perspective, and thus only by means of collective action, is it possible to keep the Earth functioning in ways that leave options open for the future. If we have duties to future generations, they bear upon us collectively, as a people. To assert that individuals should make up their own minds about such matters, implementing their own ethical leanings, is to deny that such ethical duties really exist.

Aside from possible duties to future generations there are other broad bases for interjecting ethical considerations into good land use. Many people sense religious duties to tend the land with care. For them, land use is truly good only when these duties are fulfilled. Religious belief, to be sure, is a personal matter. But it is wrong to jump from this truth to the false conclusion that religious duties are therefore inappropriate bases for public policy. Religious people are free to embrace their own ideas about good land use. They can freely advocate these ideas in the political arena, just as they can promote ethical ideals not grounded in religion. A moral claim that we should protect rare species is not somehow invalid because religious conviction lies behind it.

Along with future generations and religious beliefs is the claim that nature itself is intrinsically valuable, or that parts of nature have intrinsic value (rare species, for instance). Intrinsic value can be defined as all value possessed by nature that is unrelated to human utility. Philosophers vigorously debate whether nature can have such moral value on its own, independently of what people might think, or whether value instead can arise only when humans recognize it as such. For purposes here, in defining good land use, this distinction is unimportant. It is the ultimate moral vision that counts. If nature is valuable, then good land use ought to respect its value, whether the value is intrinsic or not. Intrinsic value in nature could reside at the level of the biotic community, requiring humans to respect the functioning of the community as such. Value could reside instead at the level of the species or (as animal welfare advocates claim) or at the level of the individual animal, particularly with animals that experience pain.

Finally, in this ethical category there are the considerations related to virtuous living. What does it mean to live a virtuous life, in terms of our interactions with nature? Does wasteful or excessive consumption amount to a defect in virtue? Is it wrong, in moral terms, to wantonly or needlessly impose suffering on other life forms or carelessly to alter lands in ways that kill plants and animals? The issue here is not the "rights" that other organisms might have. It is about people, and about what it means to live the virtuous life. A land use would be bad if it deviated from widely held notions of individual virtue.

These, then, are the major categories of ethical thinking about land (or at least one way to categorize them): approaches based on duty to future generations, religious obligations, intrinsic value, and virtue. As with the category of human utility, there is no need here to dwell on the category's many variations. *Land use will be good, for a people who recognize ethical limits (which is to say, a civilized people), only when it is consistent with their chosen ethical ideals:* that is, only (1) when it adequately fulfills duties to future generations and to nature itself; (2) when it performs felt religious obligations; and (3) when it is consistent with shared ideas about virtuous living.

Ethical ideals are highly important to people, or so public opinion studies tell us. With unusual consensus, the public perceives moral value in non-human animals and believes we should protect all species, regardless of utility.[6] People embrace other moral values, of course, unrelated to nature. We cannot assume that support for nature would consistently override these competing ideals. Still, it is just as wrong to ignore or shortchange such thinking. People take morality seriously. Land-use decisions implicate many widely accepted moral principles.

Ignorance and precaution. Any well-considered definition of good land use is almost certain to dwell at length on the first two categories of factors: on overall human utility and on the relevant ethical considerations. A third category also requires attention, although it is more elusive and it enters the equation from a different angle.

Human knowledge about nature is far from complete. Many of nature's parts are unknown or poorly understood; many processes and interactions are hard to evaluate and harder still to trace. Inevitably, decisions about land use and consumption are made behind veils of ecological ignorance. The more one learns about nature, it seems, the greater the recognition of that ignorance. Somehow, decision-making processes need to take into account this limited knowledge. It is dangerous to act based solely on what is known when that knowledge is obviously incomplete. It is even more dangerous to take major action based only on the few facts that can be empirically proven with high confidence, when countless other relevant facts are unproven or unknown. In scientific research it makes sense to insist on scientific proof; in real life it does not.

To fill in the gaps of our knowledge, hunches are required. Deep-seated intuition needs to be drawn upon. Wise land managers try to work with nature rather than against it, mimicking its ways and hoping to benefit from its built-in wisdom, even when not understood. Because mistakes are inevitable, it is prudent to leave room for second chances. When tinkering with a landscape, it is wise to save all the parts. Prudence is particularly essential in light of nature's inherent dynamism and unpredictability, which adds further layers to our ignorance.[7]

These ideas are certainly familiar to readers of serious conservation literature, where the wisdom of acting cautiously appears prominently. A common version of the idea takes the form of the so-called precautionary principle.[8] The legal mind is more inclined to phrase the same idea in terms of burdens of proof: the burden of showing harm ought to be kept reasonably low, conservationists assert, particularly when the harms that might result are grave. Would the sane person, told that he faces a 20 percent chance of getting hit by a car while crossing a street, decide to take extra precautions, or would he ignore the warning on the grounds that the chance of harm is too low or unproven?

Acting cautiously is related to one of the common legal tools used to stimulate better land-use decisions—the so-called "hard look" approach, illustrated by the National Environmental Policy Act (NEPA).[9] In its requirement for environmental impact statements, NEPA embraces a look-before-you-leap attitude toward major government actions that will alter land significantly. The federal Endangered Species Act similarly directs federal agencies to consult with the Fish and Wildlife Service before they act to learn whether their proposed activities will jeopardize the continued existence of any species.[10] More protective than these laws are the legal rules that require producers of foods and drugs to test their products thoroughly before marketing them to ensure they cause no harm.[11]

The idea of acting cautiously toward nature stimulates widely different responses. Some think the point so obviously right that debate about it seems silly. Others take a sharply opposing view, usually phrased in terms of individual liberty: people should be free to alter nature as they see fit, unless and until the evidence of harm is manifest. According to ardent defenders of liberty, the burden of proving harm should rest on those who claim that harm will occur. Some would go even further, contending that evidence of harm should take the form of scientific proof, admissible in a court of law.[12] It is worth recalling on this point the debate about Rachel Carson's classic, *Silent Spring*.[13] Carson's chief complaint was that we were acting recklessly in our uses of pesticides, and that greater caution was in order. Many of her attackers, however, overlooked or affirmatively ignored the issue of caution. Their critiques presumed that caution was entirely inappropriate, and that pesticides were properly used unless and until their overall harmfulness was fully shown. Because the evidence of harm was incomplete and (in their view) not fully persuasive, Rachel Carson was wrong to challenge what pesticide users were doing.[14]

What we have, then, are alternative ways of talking about this third category of factors relating to good land use. The issue is about human ignorance and the limits of our sensory perceptions, about the recurring errors in human reason, about the wisdom of acting cautiously given our tendency to err, and about burdens of proof. At one time we freely introduced exotic species into landscapes, unconcerned about possible harmful effects. Now we are prone to hesitate; we have suffered too many instances of these introductions gone awry. That hesitation, however we phrase it, is an important component of land-use thought. Land use is good when it avoids gambles with nature that we are ill prepared to lose. Land use is good when managers refrain from charging ahead without study, reflection, and efforts to minimize unnecessary change.

This third category of land-use factors could easily be blended into the other two. Caution in the long run could well improve human utility. Caution can also stand as a cardinal virtue or as a wise way to implement our felt ethical duties. Yet so important is this constellation of ideas, and so easy is it for the factors here to get lost, that it seems wiser to break it out for separate recognition. The ideas should stand in their own category.

These three categories—overall utility, ethical considerations, and ignorance-precaution—provide a framework for thinking about good and bad land use and hence for considering conservation's aims.

Plainly, to move beyond this three-pronged framework we would need to start making policy decisions—lots of them. At every step, in each of the three categories, alternatives are available and tough choices have to be made. Some choices, though, are far wiser than others—and the three-part framework, by identifying and distinguishing the relevant characteristics, can be of value in helping us make these determinations. An approach to land use that overlooks any of these considerations—that ignores one or even two entire categories of factors, as some do—is plainly deficient and deserves to be labeled as such.

Within conservation circles, there is hardly any issue that causes more confusion about land use, and about conservation policy overall, than the matter of science and its proper and improper roles in setting land-use policy. To take the next step in clarifying good land use, we need to address this issue. We need to consider what science is, what it can and cannot do, and how influential it ought to be in the policy arena. Sometimes science is given too much work to do. Just as often it is unduly slighted.

This issue is particularly critical today because of the tendency of many people, scientists and nonscientists alike, to want to make use of science-related terms when determining conservation goals. Ecological integrity in various forms has become one popular candidate as a land-use goal. Biological diversity and ecosystem health, variously defined, are other candidates.[15]

Why people prefer to use such science terms is not hard to figure out. Science carries prestige and an aura of objectivity. To ground a policy position in science is therefore to give it strength. Science terms also tend to incorporate a strong pronature slant, and thus they appeal to many ardent conservationists. Finally, science is technically complex in a way that elevates scientifically trained people to positions of expertise and hence authority. The more technically complex an issue, the more people are likely to turn to science to set policy. (Gifford Pinchot and other Progressive Era reformers relied on this cultural tendency a century ago to strengthen the conservation programs of the federal government.)[16]

Is it useful to talk about good land use in this way, borrowing terms from science (ecology mostly)?

Can science in fact provide the core for conservation policy? Can it provide a solid foundation for good land use?

To answer these questions we need to understand clearly what scientists are doing when they study nature. The aim of science in this setting (involving land and potential uses of it) is as essential as it is modest. Its aim is to gain understanding about nature and how it functions. It is to learn how nature works. If scientists did their jobs perfectly, they would end up knowing precisely what nature entails and how it operates in a given location. With that knowledge, one could predict accurately what nature is likely to do next, based on assumptions about outside influences. One could predict how nature would respond to particular interventions or disruptions. All of this work—and here we get to the key point—is *descriptive* in nature: it describes what nature is, how it works, and how it will work. Science, in short, describes. What science does not do, what science is incapable of doing standing alone, is to make normative judgments about the goodness or badness of nature. Science, that is, has no power to *evaluate* the land.

We confront, then, a fundamental distinction between describing nature and evaluating it normatively. To illustrate, we can consider the case of two forests, one an "old-growth" forest showing little noticeable human alteration, the other a loblolly pine plantation with trees of uniform age, aligned in rows and protected by pesticides. A scientist would describe the two forests in vastly different ways in terms of their species composition and functioning. But a scientist using only science could not pass judgment on which of the two was better. The conservationist might instinctively prefer the old-growth forest to the single-species plantation. But the grounds of that preference would not be scientific alone. What if the pine plantation so successfully met timber needs that it allowed vast forest tracts elsewhere to remain untouched? What if the pine plantation itself harbored some rare species that could not exist elsewhere? Which forest, then, would we prefer?

To say that science is purely descriptive is to say that it is unable alone to prescribe good land use. We can appreciate this point, while identifying some of science's rightful roles in land management, by comparing science with the three categories of land-use factors just distilled.

In identifying and measuring human utility, science is distinctly helpful but far from adequate for the task. Science tells us nothing about landscape aesthetics and very little about how land-use patterns might promote convenience, collegiality, and a high quality of human life. Science is on stronger ground when it comes to elements of human utility based on the consumption of food, fiber, minerals, or other elements of nature. For instance, whether particular land-use practices can or cannot produce desired resources over the long run is preeminently a science question. But whether the resources are needed is an entirely different question, based much less on science. How to make trade-offs is also not a science matter.

Many aspects of human utility depend in practice on the preferences that people embrace, individually or collectively. Science can inform our preference-setting processes, but it cannot on its own establish the preferences. The bottom line: human utility is determined by drawing extensively upon nonscientific factors.

As for ethical considerations, science has even less to say. What types of living are virtuous? What duties do we owe to future generations? Just as some questions are preeminently scientific and descriptive, others are predominately normative and nonscientific. Science can help clarify ethical choices by providing background data. When thinking about protecting rare species, for instance, we might want to know what protective steps will be required to fulfill the task, particularly when we have to decide how a duty to protect rare species stacks up against a competing moral claim. Still (and this is the bottom line here), the core reasoning on these matters is nonscientific. Science is a way to find facts, not to establish ethical norms.

Much the same conclusion is appropriate in the case of science's possible role in setting levels of caution. Science deals with the known, not with the unknown. It is a way of explaining how nature works, not whether and with what justification people ought to alter it. As with the ethical issues, science can nonetheless help greatly with the factors in this category. Scientists can articulate the limits of what we know and do not know. Scientists can present estimates of error and point out how conclusions that depend on data can change radically when new data comes in—as it does from nature, at every moment. But precaution ultimately is a prudential consideration, not a scientific fact. It is a way of dealing with ignorance and the inevitable errors in human calculations. It is not at root a principle of science.

Given these various limits on science, it ought to be clear that we cannot employ a descriptive science term (such as ecological integrity) as a normative land-use guide without first altering it substantially. We would need to augment the science in it with a good deal of ethical, prudential, and other nonscientific considerations. Only after we have done that could the term stand up as a normative land-use ideal.

There is another reason why it is vital to hold fast this distinction between describing land (the job of science) and evaluating land (largely nonscientific). Only with the distinction can we make sense of the recurring complaint that ecological integrity (and similar science terms), when used as a land-use goal, is not "good science" or is not dictated by science. The complaint goes like this: Science alone does not command that we manage lands so as to maintain their integrity. Thus, as a land-use goal, ecological integrity is not grounded in, or commanded by, sound science.

This complaint is entirely true. And it is just as entirely inapt.

Science alone does not command anything; it can never set a land-use goal, good or bad. Accordingly, no land-use goal, however phrased, can qualify as sound, unalloyed science. When ecological integrity (or biological diversity or ecosystem health) is put forth as a proposed land-use goal, the implicit claim is not that science alone commands the goal. It is that the proposed goal does a better job than any alternative in promoting good land use, in satisfying the categories of considerations that collectively compose good land use. Such a claim, of course, is laced with normative assumptions. And one could easily challenge them. But it is not relevant to dismiss the goal of ecological integrity because it is nonscientific.

This defense of ecological integrity against the charge of bad science also applies to Aldo Leopold's proposed land-use goal, land health. Leopold crafted this goal with a careful eye on the land's functioning, but he also took into account human needs, the limits of our knowledge of nature, and the errors that so often arise when people try to manipulate land excessively. Considered as Leopold proposed it—as a complex normative goal rather than as a scientific description—land health is not fairly criticized on the ground that it is bad science.

Just as the bad-science label is too quickly deployed, so, too, there is a tendency to accuse defenders of natural areas and wildness of committing a logical fallacy when they assert that we ought to preserve nature, perhaps with as little change as possible. The alleged fallacy is that these nature advocates are wrongfully jumping from the "is" of nature to the "ought" of conservation policy. Preservationists, that is, are wrongfully assuming that just because nature works in some particular way, we ought to value that as inviolable and unalterable.[17]

This is indeed a mistake in reasoning. But whether advocates of wild nature are guilty of the fallacy is by no means clear. It is, to be sure, not reasonable simply to point to unaltered or barely altered nature and use it as a land-use benchmark. Things are not that easy. We cannot designate a particular landscape or natural condition as a normative land-use standard unless we have first decided that it qualifies as, or would help promote, good land use overall. On the other hand—and here we see why nature advocates have perhaps not committed this fallacy of which they stand accused—it is entirely proper to use a given natural landscape as a benchmark for land management *after* we have done this evaluative work. Once we have defined the "ought" of good land use, carefully considering the many land-use factors, then we might legitimately point to a particular landscape or natural place and label it "good." This could happen for one or more of the various reasons already mentioned. The landscape or natural condition that we point to could have intrinsic value that we want to protect. It could be worth protecting to keep it intact for future generations or to fulfill religious obligations. It could be valuable, most of all, because of the many ways it promotes human utility.

A given landscape, occupied or unoccupied, can in fact qualify as an exemplar of good land use. Indeed, there is perhaps no more vivid way to show good land use than to find or create examples of it for people to experience.

The frustration of a good many conservationists over the cause's lack of overall direction has led to suggestions about the movement's future course. Two ideas in particular (or groups of ideas, since they take variant forms) have been put forward with regularity. They are prominent enough to be taken seriously, and we can do that by judging them in light of the land-use factors outlined above. If one or the other suggestion rates well as a normative goal, we might then take the next step and ask more practical questions about it. Can the proposed goal be presented in the public arena in a comprehensible manner, given our shallow methods of public discourse? And does it hold the potential to move the soul as well as the mind?

Conserving biological diversity. One prominent idea has been to center conservation on the reestablishment of North America's native fauna and flora, with all species, optimally, reinhabiting something like the ranges they occupied before European settlement began in earnest. This goal is sometimes talked about simply as promoting biodiversity, with the express or implicit clarification that it means biodiversity native to the continent circa 1600. Sometimes the goal is aimed more narrowly at protecting rare species, on the basis that such species are the ones most in need of care. Yet another variant of this goal is to focus on constellations of species, organized as biotic communities. The tendency again is to dwell on communities and species that are most at risk.

One vivid form of this biological goal is the call to restore big predators and other large mammals. Earth First! founder Dave Foreman has pushed the idea prominently, both in the practical work of the Wildlands Project and in his new conservation think tank, the Rewilding Institute.[18] Many conservation biologists endorse a similar focus on predators. Their point is not necessarily that predators are more valuable intrinsically than other species; rather, landscapes that have room for big predators are likely to be able to accommodate lots of other species too. Predators help keep prey species from becoming pests and degrading landscapes. When we give big predators the habitat they need, we address a number of other conservation challenges at the same time. Landscapes with big predators are enjoyable places for people to live.

How might we evaluate this idea as an overall conservation goal? To begin with, biodiversity conservation is a goal framed expressly in nonhuman terms. It is the classic statement of the much-maligned idea that conservation is about nature, not about people, and that nature needs protecting above all from human change. This is a troubling implication, and it is particularly costly when used in political debates. The goal leaves conservation open to easy criticism by its opponents, which has not been slow in coming. The goal also fosters confusion among conservationists themselves, who can easily forget, or fail to see, why biodiversity is being conserved.

As to the reasons for biodiversity conservation, few people have taken the time to work out a full answer.[19] And a full answer, publicly articulated, is needed if the goal is to be used broadly. An outline of a full answer would likely go something like this: Biodiversity ought to be conserved for quite a list of reasons. Most obvious are the ethical ones, having to do with intrinsic value and duties to future generations. Less obvious but more weighty are the ways that protecting biodiversity promotes human utility, broadly defined. To protect biodiversity is necessarily to protect a wide range of ecological processes and functions. It is to keep waterways clean and reasonably natural in flow, for instance, and to keep soil mostly in place. When these ecological functions are protected and a rather full array of native species do thrive in a given place, then the landscape is more likely to be a good for humans, too. Biodiversity protection, that is, can be used as a placeholder or a management parameter to keep conservation aimed so that it succeeds in generating a suite of human benefits. To keep all the parts is also a good precautionary measure, thus rating high in the third category of land-use factors.

One problem with biodiversity protection used this way is that most people have real trouble tracing its links to human welfare. It is simply not obvious that when we promote wild species we benefit people at the same time. The links are present, of course. But the connections for most people are too indirect and too easily challenged. Why be so indirect? If biodiversity promotes healthy lands, then why not talk about the healthy lands directly? And if healthy lands in turn are important because they supply good benefits for people, why not talk more openly about these human advantages?

The big problem with focusing on biodiversity, then, is this: it forces people to fill in the gaps left by unarticulated reasoning. It forces users on their own to connect biodiversity to the land's functioning, and then to connect the land's functioning to human welfare and to such matters as ethical living and the wisdom of precaution. To use biodiversity as a freestanding goal is to expect ordinary people to learn and appreciate the many ways that biodiversity can help them. Some people gravitate toward the goal without much thought. For more dubious audiences the goal is a demanding one intellectually. A person needs to think deeply about how biodiversity conservation can promote sound overall land use. When a person does not take time to do that, or when the intellectual steps and connections are just not seen, then biodiversity looks far less appealing as a prime goal. It becomes easy to agree that biodiversity advocates care only about wildlife, not about people. The misanthropy label can stick.

Another main problem with biodiversity conservation as a goal is that it leaves open the question of spatial scale. Do we merely want all wild species to exist somewhere, or do want them to return to all the places they once inhabited? The two answers are quite different. Neither charts a very sensible path.

If our goal is simply to keep species from becoming extinct, then we could successfully achieve it and still suffer massive declines in our natural landscapes. We could create biodiversity reserves or zoos, even as biodiversity continues to decrease in all the human-occupied places. Defined in this way, biodiversity protection would do little to sustain the places where people live.

If we choose the other option, pushing to reestablish wild species everywhere, we encounter equally severe problems. To adopt this more ambitious approach to biodiversity is essentially to embrace a wilderness model of conservation policy. We can restore all species to their pre-European settlement ranges only if we sharply reduce human numbers and dramatically change our ways of living. For conservationists, this proposal would be politically fatal. It suggests—indeed, it verily trumpets—that conservationists prefer to have as few people as possible on the land. The political backlash would be severe. The wilderness model is also problematic for another reason. When wilderness is the goal, we have no solid basis for deciding which human alterations are acceptable and which are not. All human changes are degrading, differing only in degree. When all change is bad, how do we compromise?

Land is well used when it satisfies a wide range of human needs. In the wilderness vision of conservation, those needs are not being met. Wilderness is thus not an example of good land use, all things considered. It is merely a component or fragment of good land use; merely a piece (albeit a critical one) of a larger landscape where people live and meet their basic needs.

Presumably, the rationale for using a wilderness-type conservation goal is because we do not really expect ever to achieve it. Trade-offs will be made. Other groups will look after the human-utility considerations, while conservationists stand up for the wild things. Rather than promote an integrated vision of humans in nature, conservationists could maintain a narrow, specialty focus in their advocacy—on wild nature. Conservationists can defend wildness; other people can look after more immediate human concerns. Things will then get sorted out in the crucibles of public sentiment and public policy making.

This line of reasoning is plausible enough, but the costs of it are high—too high. When biodiversity is the banner cause—and especially when the aim is to restore all species to their native ranges—conservation is wide open to all of the now-familiar critiques: it is elitist, misanthropic, impractical, and so on. More than that, biodiversity provides precious little guidance for conservation activists themselves in determining which land alterations are worse than others. It simply makes little sense to judge competing land uses based solely on their effects on wild species. Too many relevant factors are left out. Biodiversity concerns need to be subsumed into something larger. They need to be part of a more encompassing conservation goal that includes the full range of land-use factors.

Ecological restoration. A second goal being pushed today to bring focus to conservation efforts is the call to engage in ecological restoration. Here the work of William Jordan stands out, particularly his recent synthesis and call to arms, *The Sunflower Forest.*[20] Restoration is an effort to heal land in natural terms. It is a plan to undo much of the change that humans have wrought so that lands more closely resemble their former conditions.

Some restorationists hope to return lands as much as possible to the conditions they were in before European settlers arrived. Others see that goal as impossible, preferring instead a less ambitious version. They call for renaturalizing a landscape, or revitalizing it, using locally wild species when possible but without attempting an exact match to any historical era. One reason why an exact match is impossible is because nature changes on its own. Thus, to return land to its "natural" condition we cannot simply mimic its condition circa 1600, even if that were possible. Even without humans around (and they were around in 1600), the land would have changed. Restoration's target is inevitably in motion.

In Jordan's view, restoration is a particularly attractive conservation ethic because the work that it requires, when done locally by local people, provides good opportunities to get people out on the land. It allows local people to interact, to work together, to learn about the land, to help heal it, and, one hopes, to gain a deep-seated respect and love for it. For Jordan, this last benefit is just as important as the practical work to heal the land. Long-term conservation requires a citizenry that values healthy, natural lands. Restoration ecology, therefore, can work on two levels at once: healing lands and promoting a culture of conservation.[21]

What, then, should we make of ecological restoration as a goal? How does it rate? When we start probing restoration, we find that it shares many of the defects of biodiversity and big-predator conservation. Explicit in the ethic of restoration is the belief that human-wrought change is bad, and the less there is of it the better. The charge of misanthropy, therefore, is just as strong here. Even the language of restoration is rather troubling: to restore is to undo, which is to say to reverse all the bad things that people have done to land. If a particular human land use is plainly a bad one, the message can make good sense. But what if a community is turning an ordinary wheat field back into a prairie? What is the message then? That wheat fields are bad? That agricultural land uses are bad? That people inevitably degrade land, even when they grow crops to eat?

As in the case of biodiversity, ecological restoration standing alone shows too little awareness of human needs. It supplies no basis for judging the merits of land-use trade-offs. A more mild form of restoration would seek to keep lands as natural as possible when they are not being intensively used by people. That idea is plainly worthy. But what does mild restoration really accomplish? Does it achieve much ecologically when it merely involves small tracts here and there? And are restorationists doing any more than seizing the leftover scraps of land after the bigger land-use players have fed at the banquet?

When used as an overall conservation ideal, restoration is problematic because it is an exclusive land use, or nearly so. Restored areas provide few or no places where people can live and grow food. People visit restored tracts but do not stay. If restored places do contribute to human welfare other than for recreation, it is because they promote the ecological well-being of their surrounding landscapes. Yet, the language of restoration has no good way to talk about these larger landscapes and about the ecological connections between restored places and nonrestored places.[22] Only indirectly and in poorly explained ways is restoration linked to the functioning of human-occupied lands.[23]

These two broad approaches, biodiversity protection and natural-area restoration, are attractive because they appeal to the hearts and souls of many people (and, of course, because they do involve important work). And therein lies the key to their popularity. Compared with sustainability they are positively enlivening, particularly the work of reviving big fauna. But their grave defects remain. In the end, both goals tend to drag conservation down when they are promoted as freestanding goals. Both goals are open to the charge of favoring nature over people. Neither supplies much guidance for the hardest work of conservation. Neither, moreover, is particularly useful in responding to the cultural criticisms that conservation faces about liberty, private property, equality, and the like.

When Aldo Leopold wrote about conservation in his "Farmer as a Conservationist," he brought matters down to the level of the individual landowner and phrased them colloquially. Conservation came about when land did well by its owner and when the owner did well by his land. In this much-quoted phrase and others like it, Leopold linked conservation to the satisfaction of human needs—feeding the farm family and providing shelter and heat. At the same time, the owner was expected to maintain the land's ecological health, its beauty, and, if at all feasible, its rare species.

When Leopold talked about conservation being good for the land he principally had in mind lands that humans had already degraded. Yet even lands put to ordinary use could gain in ecological health and beauty. Human use could make them more fertile, productive, and biologically diverse. When conservation is understood this way, the human actor plays a more honorable, beneficial role. Restoration-style conservation does entail making lands better, with people as the agents of change. But the end point of restoration typically is to heal lands and then set them aside. They become places that people might visit, but not places for them to live. What Leopold had in mind was quite different and more ambitious. He was not out to restore entire biological communities that had no people in them. He sought to promote the health and beauty of landscapes where people lived and worked.

The conservation movement needs a message that shows people as positive agents of improvement, not merely sources of degradation. And it needs a benchmark for good land use, plainly constructed in such a way that human needs are taken seriously and satisfied insofar as possible, not shunted to the side for others to worry about. To ignore human needs and merely champion nature is to erect a policy framework in which conservation is opposed to humans. And to a large extent, this is where we are today. When conservation cares only for nature while other social entities look out for people, conflict is inevitable. The trade-offs begin. Yet it is far from clear that in the United States trade-offs really are needed. It is far from clear that to feed and clothe ourselves we really need to relinquish our felt ethical obligations toward nature or to diminish the land's long-term fertility. No doubt conservation does clash with profligate living and with unbridled individual liberty. But it brings many good things as well.

To succeed in a serious way, conservation needs to offer an alluring vision of what life could be like if people embraced conservation ideas. It needs to offer an entire package, just as Leopold did in the single-farm setting in his "Farmer as a Conservationist." With his vision of the corn-belt farm years into the future, Leopold responded to the desire of his farm audience to witness, on the ground, what his conservation message was all about. Conservationists today need to follow this example, coming up with more of them, adapting them to contemporary scenes, extending them to suburbs and cities, and otherwise talking about the good things that conservation can bring. Conservation is not just about living responsibly. It is about health, beauty, strong communities, vibrant life, and ways of living that yield deep satisfaction.

CHAPTER 6

Conservation's Core Tasks

T he foregoing chapters, expressly and by implication, have patched together a catalogue of work tasks that await the conservation movement's attention. The list is rather long, much of it dealing with the knotty challenge of fostering a nature-respecting culture. Indeed, one reason why the conservation movement today is so fragmented is precisely because the job list is so long. Busy working on the specific pieces, few conservationists give thought to the whole and thus to the matter of priorities.[1]

Can we sensibly pare down this working list? Can we identify the overriding conservation tasks, especially the ones that require concerted action if conservation writ large is to prosper?

It is unlikely that we shall ever see an end to the need for scientific research into how land functions and how human activities affect nature's systems. Also never-ending is the need to counter conservation's critics, especially the confused and confusing rhetoric that comes packaged in economic, libertarian, and technocratic jargon. Then, too, conservation is possible only when democracy functions effectively, and democracy, we know too well, is susceptible to many ailments. Whenever big money rules the political roost, conservation flounders. Campaign-finance reform is essential, and so is the revitalization of senses of citizenship and true citizen rule.

Without discounting the importance of such work, it is nonetheless possible to highlight six particular tasks that rise above the rest in their overall importance and in the need for orchestrated action to implement them. Together they supply an intellectual agenda for the cause of land conservation.

An overall goal. Agenda item number one, already flagged, is the movement's need to clarify its goal, its overall vision of harmoniously living on the land. The goal needs to be one that plainly promotes good land use, broadly defined.[2] It needs to portray people as having a rightful place on the land, not as aliens. And it needs to define success so that it includes human flourishing as well as ecologically healthy lands. For the goal to work, the movement as a whole, or a sizeable part of it, will need to employ it regularly in rhetoric and action. A goal that lacks widespread support is unlikely to reorient public thinking about the cause.

An updated version of Aldo Leopold's goal, land health, is a likely candidate and deserves consideration. Ecosystem health, a variant, has its own proponents and also deserves a look.[3] The latter term borrows a word from the realm of science, thereby linking the goal to ecology. But the word *ecosystem* is not popularly known and it arrives with awkward baggage. Many scientists deny that ecosystems really exist as places, given the difficulty of deciding where one ecosystem ends and the next begins.[4] Indeed, an ecosystem is better defined as a set of ecological relationships rather than as a distinct physical place. Given this technical problem, it seems wise to stay away from the term. Leopold's preferred term, *land,* is a familiar, nontechnical word and is not weakened by any scientific disputes. The difficulty with this term is that it works well only if, like Leopold, we give the term a broad definition, so that it encompasses waters, plants, animals, and people, as well as rocks and soils. It would take a deliberate, concerted effort by conservationists to broaden the term's meaning in this way. Still, we already speak of our "homeland" and of being the "land of the free"—uses of the term that are not dissimilar. With enough work, the broader definition could take hold.

As for the term *health,* it conveys positive connotations. It also escapes the problems of being a technical, elitist word. Indeed, so positive are the word's connotations that it is hard to imagine anyone arguing against it. President G. W. Bush saw rhetorical value in the phrase *forest health* when pushing his plan to accelerate harvesting western timber. The conservation movement might take his cue. Yes, we want healthy forests, along with healthy farmlands and healthy suburbs. So what would it mean for a particular landscape to be truly healthy, and how can we promote it? They are good questions to ask.

One alleged problem with land health as a goal is that the term is scientifically inaccurate. Health, some observers claim, is an attribute only of an individual organism.[5] Land can be healthy only if it is so tightly integrated as to constitute an organism. The scientific evidence, though, shows otherwise, that lands are more dynamic and their composition more fluid. A shifting web of life cannot really be healthy.

The flaw in this complaint is that it defines health too narrowly. In common speech health is used more broadly than that, as in "community health" and "health of the economy." Health denotes a state of affairs that is flourishing and properly functioning, free of disease or serious defect. To speak of healthy land is thus an accurate usage of the term.

A more substantial challenge to land health is the difficulty of grounding the term in science and sound policy. When used as a normative ideal, land health goes beyond science to take into account a range of human interests. Moreover, people are part of the land, which means lands can be fully healthy only when they satisfy human needs. Leopold talked about wilderness areas as examples of healthy land, and they are, in the sense that they flourish ecologically. But wilderness areas lack people, and thus the health of them does not include the notion of human needs. More broadly useful are Leopold's other examples of healthy lands—the long-used pastoral landscapes that people have tended in ways that satisfied Leopold's basic definition. These landscapes did include people.[6]

Before unveiling land health as a preeminent goal, the conservation cause would need to do its scientific homework. It must draw together what is known about the land's functioning and distill its key ecological elements. Deliberately and thoughtfully it needs to synthesize what ecologists know about the land and then transform that synthesis into a vision of people living on the land. Land health should be based on good ecological science, but needs to go well beyond that to become a fully formed vision of harmonious life. Once formulated, a sound goal could provide guidance for making decisions about individual land parcels, without dictating precise uses. It could also provide guidelines for mixing land uses at larger spatial scales.

A variant on land health is the idea of ecological integrity, which ecologists have crafted as a way to describe intact natural communities, ones that retain their natural composition and key ways of functioning.[7] As a conservation goal, however, ecological integrity has defects, including those that plague biodiversity conservation and ecological restoration. As scientists use the term, ecological integrity describes a natural community that has few or no people in it. The needs of humans play no role in the term's definition, and human changes to the land are at best neutral. This hostility to humans is strongest when ecological integrity is measured at small spatial scales. Consider a thousand-acre wheat field, so crucial to feeding people. Because the field will lack the full range of native species, plant and animal, it will lack integrity. Yet, it makes little sense to condemn the wheat field as bad land use without considering the larger context. Humans simply cannot dwell on lands without diminishing their integrity in this pure sense. An additional, more technical problem is that ecological integrity was developed to aid in the narrow, descriptive work of science and is being proposed to fill a much different, normative role.

Too much conservation work is now performed without adequate thought about how it all fits together. Collectively, the conservation cause has little or nothing in the way of an overall goal. Tract-by-tract preservation work too often unfolds with little concern about larger ecological landscapes. Specific policies are promoted with hardly any regard for how the work of one group relates to the work of another. This needs to change. Without coherence and cohesion, the conservation cause will continue to flounder, particularly when addressing urban sprawl, habitat fragmentation, and other landscape-scale problems.

A vision of private land ownership. What should it mean for a person to own land and other parts of nature (water flows, mines, animals)? What legal rights should an owner possess, particularly to act in ways that frustrate sound conservation? With 60 percent of the nation in private hands, few issues are more important.[8]

Questions about private ownership form the core of perhaps the greatest land conservation challenge of our age: how to get the private landowner to use land conservatively, while treating taxpayers fairly and while sustaining the core economic and civic functions that private property so effectively provides.

Over the years, conservationists have used a variety of tools to push, encourage, cajole, or enjoin landowners to act in ways more aligned with conservation. Lately, the movement has become comfortable with the idea of paying landowners money, with little recognition of the dangers of doing so. This solution can take the form of annual payments under government programs. Money is also paid under longer-term programs that involve the purchase of conservation easements or development rights. Rarely do discussions about payment programs mention their unfairness to taxpayers, for whom conservation becomes, at the personal level, involuntary. (When private donations are used the payments are voluntary but still unfair given the gross mismatch of costs and benefits; would it be fair to expect volunteers to fund public schools or national defense?) There is also little express attention given to the effects that payments have on landowners who are conserving without getting paid (the only truly voluntary conservation) and on landowners who would conserve voluntarily did they not see neighbors taking money. When payment becomes the norm, it seems foolish for a person to conserve without getting paid.

The root of the problem is this: payment programs tell landowners, loud and clear, that conservation is a voluntary activity, not an expectation of ownership. They keep the obligations of ownership low while calling into question the legitimacy of regulatory programs that force landowners to conserve without getting paid. If landowners in one county get paid to refrain from destructive practices, why should landowners in the next be forced to do it for free? Where is the fairness in that?

The whole matter of private ownership and private lands conservation is a complex one, more so than conservationists have acknowledged. A coherent platform is needed, one that addresses the full range of issues. What can we reasonably expect of landowners? When would incentive payments be fair, to owners and taxpayers, and when is regulation more appropriate? Both tools presumably have roles to play, but at the moment they are being used haphazardly.

A coherent use of these tools should build upon a thoughtful inquiry into the legal rights that landowners ought to possess. What rights should be theirs, and what duties should they bear to act in ways consistent with the common good? When the law defines landowner rights, should nature play a bigger role, in the sense that an owner's rights vary from parcel to parcel based on differing soils, slopes, drainage, vegetation, climate, and animal life? The answers are indispensable. At the moment, though, the only people asking the questions are opponents of conservation. And their answers are predictable: landowners should have the right pretty much to do as they please, with nature irrelevant, and when conservation is needed the public should pay for it.

Looming on the horizon is the whole matter of how extensive landowner development rights should be.[9] As much as other Americans, conservationists assume that landowners have the inherent right to develop. They therefore avoid the issue. That silence is a huge mistake, the product of intellectual laziness, institutional fragmentation, and a simple lack of courage. A growing number of land-use laws already curtail the right to develop—laws protecting wetlands and floodplains, for instance. One day we may awaken and realize that private property is a product of law and that property laws, like all other laws, are subject to legislative change. There is no constitutional barrier to a massive redefinition of landowner rights.

The right to develop could be pruned severely in ways that treat landowners fairly and have no particularly negative effect on the economy. The United States could do what Great Britain did in 1947 (and what other countries have also done)—transform the "right" to develop into more of a privilege. The idea may seem unreasonable, but that is only because we have not studied private property as an institution. We have failed to see that private property is not an individual right first and foremost but rather a tool used by society to foster the common good. We have also neglected to think clearly about the market value of development rights. When vacant land rises in value due to its development potential, the enhanced value is not attributable to anything the landowner has done. The local community or society at large is responsible for the higher value.[10] The landowner is merely the lucky beneficiary—or at least this is so under the present system, which allows the landowner to capture this communally created asset. But why should the value belong to the landowner? Why should a landowner be able to sit back and watch the value of his or her land go from $500 per acre to $5,000 or $25,000 per acre and then step forward and claim that profit? That is the system as we understand it. Having considered nothing else, we assume that ownership inherently entails this right. But it does not, and it need not.

In a recent essay, law professor Joseph Sax has usefully distilled our essential dilemma on this issue of development rights.[11] Good land use will require many acres to remain free of substantial development. But which acres will be left undeveloped, when the possibilities are often many? If we really wanted to treat all landowners fairly, we would decide in advance the level of permissible development in a landscape and then calibrate the development rules accordingly. We would arrange things legally so that all landowners shared pro rata in the benefits of permissible development while development occurred only in places where it was appropriate, ecologically and socially. But we do not do that, of course. And we do not do it because we are reluctant to plan ahead. We are reluctant to tell landowners they may not develop until the problems being caused are readily apparent. By that point, however, substantial development has taken place (often in the wrong locations), and the regulatory brakes have to be applied hard, halting nearly all further development. Landowners who have already developed enjoy the benefits; landowners who waited are now subject to severe constraints. It is an unfair system, to be sure. Yet it exists, Sax tells us, mostly because prodevelopment interests are in charge of the system. Progrowth interests resist forward-looking land planning. By doing so, they keep in place an approach to land-use controls that inevitably produces unfairness. As for the resulting claims of unfairness, Sax observes, it is hard to be sympathetic when the people doing the complaining have largely brought the problem on themselves.

When the conservation movement does finally get serious about property rights, it should pay special attention to the public's ownership interests in two key parts of nature: water and wildlife.[12] For generations, courts have made clear that the public possesses expansive legal rights in these elements. Individual owners, in the case of water, possess merely *use* rights, which are subject to the public's superior legal title and which can be exercised only in ways that are socially reasonable and beneficial. Wild animals are similarly owned by the public, even when they are found on private land. Were our legal system to take seriously these public rights, protecting them securely, our understanding of private land rights would change dramatically. We would recognize that the public has legitimate interests in the ways all private property is used, particularly property rights in nature. Early in our country's history, courts routinely proclaimed that private property rights were subject to legal restraint when they clashed with the public's rights.[13] Such reasoning is unfamiliar to us these days. We assume that only individuals have rights. But the legal record says otherwise, particularly in the case of water, waterways, and wildlife. The conservation cause needs to revive and deploy these legal ideas.

Crafting mechanisms for collective action. Many conservation problems can be addressed only by means of remedial actions taken at a level well above the individual citizen or landowner. Local community action (zoning and public health rules, for instance) is sometimes wide-ranging enough to get the job done. Increasingly, though, action on state, national, or even international scales is necessary because the problems are so broad. Nature is intricately interconnected, and market forces operate without borders. If some conservation problems arise because of a poorly managed natural commons—the tragedy of the commons, made famous by Garrett Hardin—just as many are the result of the opposite situation: because landscapes have been carved into pieces too small for the owner or manager to use responsibly. This is the so-called tyranny of small decisions, or tragedy of fragmentation.[14] No one acting alone can sensibly protect a river, clean up mercury-laced air, or preserve enough wildlife habitat to keep a mobile species alive. Without good methods of collective action—and strong senses of citizenship and democracy to undergird such action—conservation will remain unable to remedy large-scale problems.

The need for collective action has hardly gone unnoticed. Ecosystem management, another vague conservation concept, is based on the recognition that parcel-by-parcel work is inadequate.[15] The idea of community-based conservation is founded on the same wisdom.[16] Step by step, we are recognizing the need to craft mechanisms for making land-use decisions at levels well above the individual parcel. Sound mechanisms would likely be organized around natural features such as catchment basins rather than along arbitrary political lines. Yet, this means creating whole new types of government intervention—at a time when antigovernment sentiment runs high. Resistance will no doubt remain strong.

The people most affected by new conservation rules—primarily landowners—would of course need to be involved in any governance scheme. But they cannot be left to do the work alone. Landowners are economically interested parties. Collectively they have accumulated a rather disturbing record of ignoring people downstream and downwind while degrading the integrity of ecological systems. The frequent assertion that landowners know best—and have the most at stake—is only partly true. And the truth that it contains is often offset by the tendency of landowners to construct their own versions of "What's good for General Motors is good for America."

Conservation requires coordinated action. This is true despite the laments of moralists that we are too quick to blame the system for our problems instead of shouldering responsibility ourselves. In the case of land use, the system *does* deserve much of the blame. Good land use would be far easier to achieve if our systems were reformed. Indeed, without such reformation, many conservation projects are nearly—or even completely—impossible. The predicament is easy to explain in economic terms. The individual who practices conservation generates benefits that flow to the community, while the costs all accrue to the individual. There is thus a mismatch of costs and benefits, which can be remedied only when everyone works together. Even without this economic theory, though, it is quite evident that many landowners misuse lands because the market pressures them to do so or because good land use is impractical or futile. If I refrain from building a house in the green space around the city, thereby showing my support for open space, what good have I done when other people build instead? Either everyone restrains or nothing is accomplished.

Sound decision-making processes are not easy to erect. Making the challenge harder are the well-fueled suspicions people have about government and the fact that governments are increasingly dominated by money. The conservation cause has no choice but to attack the problem head-on, doing all it can to revive true democracy and responsible citizenship. In a recent work, *The Last Refuge: Patriotism, Politics, and the Environment in an Age of Terror,* David Orr presents that situation as clearly and forcefully as anyone could: "There are some things that can be done only by an alert citizenry acting with responsible and democratically controlled governments. Only governments moved by an ethically robust and organized citizenry can act to ensure the fair distribution of wealth within and between generations. Only governments prodded by their citizens can act to limit risks posed by technology or clean up the mess afterward. Only governments and an environmentally literate public can choose to adopt and enforce standards that move us toward a cradle-to-cradle materials policy."[17] We are afflicted with bad politics, Orr tells us, which is aggravated by faulty senses of patriotism and civic duty. Probusiness interests have exacerbated our condition by labeling government as the enemy of liberty and incompetent to boot. Politically bruised and lethargic, almost drugged by the entertainment industry, we need to awaken as citizens.

The conservation cause needs to use particular force in countering the claim that conservation laws interfere with individual liberty. It is simply not true, all things considered. When government protects our air, our water, our wildlife, our children, it *increases* our liberties. When we gather together to make rules for our shared landscapes, we *exercise* one of our most important, positive liberties. When we adopt public policies that provide for future generations, we act upon our ethical ideals, freely embraced.

Arrogance, ignorance, and burdens of proof. Our assessment of good land use has teased out for independent attention the whole matter of ignorance and factual uncertainty. So important is this issue, however, and so deeply does it pervade conservation disputes, that the movement ought to position it in the front rank of high-priority issues. Conservation needs good ways to talk about this ignorance and well-crafted proposals to accommodate it.

Given our vast ignorance about nature, we ought to act cautiously when tampering with it. The idea could hardly be more simple. Look before you leap, the old wisdom had it (though we need to do more than just look). The United States, of course, has a long-standing habit of leaping without looking, or leaping after no more than a quick glance. Even our glances have been made through the distorting lens of hope, ambition, and greed. Still, as scientific knowledge has grown, so, too, has our awareness of how much we do not know. So many and extended are the ecological ripples flowing from even a single act that no person could conceivably trace them. Caution makes sense. Leaving room to correct mistakes makes sense.

Given the legalism of American culture these days, the conservation cause might best address this issue in the same way that lawyers do, in terms of burdens of proof about potential harms. Should those who alter nature be expected to show in advance that they will cause no harm? Or, instead, should critics bear the burden of showing that harm will likely ensue? Aside from *who* bears the burden, there is the question about *what* it should be. How much evidence must we have about a potential problem before deciding that remedial action is appropriate? In the normal civil trial, the case is won by the side that presents the greater amount (the preponderance) of the evidence. In criminal trials, we expect prosecutors to do much better than that—to offer proof beyond a reasonable doubt. Various other burden levels exist in the law, both higher and lower.

Within the scientific community there is considerable reluctance to give specific meaning to the idea of proof. Scientists prefer incontrovertible evidence but often settle for less because they must. More to the point, science (to reiterate) is merely a fact-finding and descriptive enterprise. Science as such gives no guidance on what we should do with our scientific data once we have compiled it. Nor can science tell us how much data we should assemble before taking action. When is the evidence about a possible problem sufficient to merit a response? That is a policy question, not a scientific one.

It is hard to know what policy stances would emerge if the conservation cause took time to study this issue carefully. We could decide that caution is variously appropriate, depending upon circumstantial factors. Differing burdens of proof might apply in different settings.

No conservation issue better highlights the confusion here than the various planetary alterations collectively known as global climate change. To the developed world generally, available evidence is more than adequate to demonstrate the existence of a severe problem meriting action. In the United States, however, the debate drones on. It does so not chiefly because scientific opinion is significantly divided, but because the debating parties employ such diverse presumptions about the amount of proof needed to decide that a problem in fact exists. How much evidence do we need before acting on an apparent problem? In dealing with terrorist threats we demand very little and we are willing to use any shreds of data that come our way. What should the corresponding standard be in the case of climate change?

Conservation and social justice. Conservative land use is complexly linked with questions of social justice and fair access to the material substances that support human life. In a world where true justice prevailed, conservation would be easier. Having said that, however, our environmental problems are too urgent to delay action until the distant day when social ills are gone. Conservation cannot wait. In any case, sound conservation work is very likely to improve social justice rather than the reverse. If that is so, then the need for conservation–social justice trade-offs is probably not very great.

The conservation cause urgently needs a coherent platform regarding social justice. That platform should include two components: (1) to address the ways conservation can improve social justice; and (2) to include specific remedial proposals that take effect when conservation measures do actually make social problems worse.

Conservation groups have come under attack for ignoring issues of environmental justice.[18] The complaint is accurate insofar as it identifies a gap in the work of many groups. At the same time, it is often unfair in that it fails to recognize why conservation groups have spent their resources as they have. It is not enough for critics to show that social justice is important; they need to demonstrate why efforts to promote it deserve a higher priority than other work that environmental groups are now doing.

National groups have sufficient money to address only a handful of peculiarly local problems, and most environmental justice disputes are local. To residents of a particular neighborhood, success in an environmental dispute can come when a waste dump, toxic emitter, or other undesirable land use is pushed into someone else's backyard. From a national perspective, this may hardly qualify as success at all. As national groups see things, it is better to use resources to stop the waste generation or pollution at its source. Then the bad land use will go nowhere.

The most acute social justice issue today is the growing inequality in income and wealth that characterizes America. Our tendency has been to address this inequality by growing the economic pie larger rather than changing the "free" market system. For conservation, this grow-the-pie approach is highly troublesome because it plays into the hands of opponents. So long as the nation has tens of millions of poor people, critics can discredit new conservation measures whenever they raise prices for food, transportation, or shelter. These worries about the poor can appear decidedly disingenuous when uttered by conservation opponents who apparently care about the poor only when they provide shields to protect business as usual. Still, the claims have merit. It is not a good outcome when conservation policies make life even harder for poor people.

One response is to point out that market prices are notoriously inaccurate as indicators of true cost. Sticker prices on products are routinely low because they discount the land's degradation, downplay human health, and ignore the future. A conservation measure that forces producers to consider these costs, thereby raising the sticker price of a commodity, can nonetheless make the overall true costs of producing the commodity go down. But this answer is not enough. When conservation measures do make basic commodities more expensive at the cash register, they need to be accompanied by mechanisms that offset the higher prices.

Ways of achieving this kind of economic equalization are not hard to identify. Higher commodity prices can be joined with changes in government programs (taxation or welfare schemes, for instance) so as to offset the costs for poor people while still providing incentive to conserve. For instance, a dollar-per-gallon gas tax might be accompanied by removing an employee's Social Security tax on the first $5,000 of earned income, with the gas revenues then added to the Social Security fund. Similar adjustments in other programs could also be made, in ways that are tax neutral and do not undercut conservation gains. In some instances it might be possible for the economic gains that conservation generates to be used directly to counterbalance the losses (for instance, land preservation measures that significantly raise values of surrounding lands; these land-value gains could be captured and turned over to those who suffer losses). In any case, it is not particularly hard to devise tax-neutral ways to offset higher prices for the poor. The hard part is to muster the political will. Many equalization tools would be politically inconceivable today. Still, conservationists would be wise to propose the measures, just to make clear that, if we choose, we can promote conservation without making social problems worse.

The conservation community needs to develop an overall position on this issue. It needs a platform that recognizes justice concerns and explains how we can address them. To a large extent (and this point bears repeating), environmental laws correct defects in market pricing. What the cash register displays as an increase in prices is often better explained as the elimination of an unfair, destructive subsidy—the kind of subsidy that comes when a commodity producer is legally allowed to impose costs on people downwind, downstream, or in the future. To end a subsidy (and a right to pollute is plainly a subsidy) is to improve the market's functioning.

History and environmental change. When Americans argue about history, it is largely because something vital is at stake. History relates how we got to where we are today as a people. It is the narrative and explanatory tale of our collective successes and failures. Inevitably, history books reflect the eras when they were written and the personal leanings of the authors. True objectivity is not possible. At worst, history can be positively distorted to promote a historian's personal agenda. A historian who claims that good historical outcomes were caused by particular public policies and historical forces necessarily implies that we ought to continue those policies and forces if we wish to enjoy even more of the good results. In the same way, for a historian to explain why American society has failed in the past is to assert that we ought to reform the cultural elements or public policies that led to our failures.

The conservation cause has paid little attention to history, including the history of conservation efforts themselves. Busy with daily work, it has made little effort to promote sound histories and shows no particular interest in challenging bad ones. And bad ones, alas, abound.

As conservation's market-oriented critics tell the story, our nation's environmental progress has had little or nothing to do either with government regulation or with the work of environmental organizations. Progress has come about instead largely through the invisible hand of the market. As the country has gotten wealthier, it has been able to afford a better environment, which is, critics assert, mostly just another commodity or service to be chosen from among the market's many offerings.[19] Also bringing environmental improvement has been the miracle known as private property.[20] When nature is put in private hands (it is said), people take care of what they own. As property rights are more precisely defined and as more of nature becomes privately owned, our environmental condition improves even more. An embarrassing fact here, for proponents of this view, is that American businesses often have rather abysmal environmental records when they operate overseas, free of American laws. Not an issue, though, according to conservation's critics. It merely shows that America is wealthier, and because of our wealth we insist in our country that businesses clean up their acts.

This is an interesting narrative but not at all well supported. To be sure, there is a rough correlation in industrialized and industrializing countries between wealth and environmental condition. But correlation and causation are entirely different matters. Probably a stronger correlation exists between two other factors: environmental conditions in a country and its level of liberal democracy. The United States has had periods of conspicuous income growth when environmental conditions rapidly worsened (the late nineteenth century and the 1950s, to cite two examples).[21] Economic growth, it would seem, improves the environment only when the new wealth is used to curtail environmentally degrading practices. But why would businesses spend their wealth that way? Why would individuals do so in their daily lives? It is not enough to say that people in a wealthier country demand healthier, more beautiful surroundings. Some of them do; many of them do not. But even for those who do, how do they make their demands known and how does environmental change come about?

The stories told by conservation's critics typically display an astonishing confusion of cause and effect. Indeed, to the extent that there is a *causal* relationship between wealth and environmental improvement, it could just as well work in the opposite direction in the United States today. It is environmental improvement that causes the wealth, not the reverse. Surely there is a causal connection between improvements in sanitation and clean drinking water and increases in worker productivity. When soil is fertile and uncontaminated, it is likely to yield crops of greater nutritional value, thereby improving individual health and worker strength.

The conservation movement ought to be taking on these issues vigorously. It should seek out accurate historical accounts about how we have come to where we are in environmental terms. Sound accounts are likely to note the importance of collective action in public and private spheres.[22] Pollution control, surely, has occurred largely because polluters have been forced to cut back by government mandate, which in turn has resulted from citizen action. Those who doubt this fact need only look at where the laws are in effect today and where the pollution still takes place. Pollution goes down when laws mandate it. Pollution largely continues when no law is imposed or no strong social norm is brought to bear. Water pollution illustrates the point. Starting three decades ago, federal pollution law told point-source water polluters to cut back, while it left other pollution sources (polluted runoff from land uses) largely to discretionary programs of the states. The result today: point-source pollution has dramatically declined, while non-point-source pollution continues apace. But even such evidence would seem unneeded. One only needs to study the political arenas and watch polluters and land developers as they fight tooth and nail to avoid curtailing their nature-degrading activities. If market processes alone are leading them to ever-higher levels of environmental responsibility, then why do they resist? If greater wealth automatically leads to healthier land, why do our wetlands, barrier islands, and riparian corridors keep disappearing the more our economy grows? If greater wealth is good for the environment, why do we keep adding species to the endangered list and why do we spend money on deathbed recovery plans? And what about the potent pesticides that were killing birds and other creatures wholesale in the 1950s and 1960s? Plainly, the wealthier we got, the more birds that were killed—until new laws, pushed by citizens, brought about change. Perhaps it is democracy that produces good environmental outcomes, and wealth is important chiefly to the extent that it promotes citizen governance.

In thinking about environmental change, it is unwise to discount the nonlegal tools that have brought about environmental improvement. Laws have not done everything. Social norms and public expectations have played a role. But here, too, the work of conservation organizations is visibly present. If public pressure leads a Ford Motor Company to improve its gas mileage ratings, can we tell the full story without mentioning the conservation groups that raised the issue, day after day, and insisted repeatedly that the company clean up its act? It is simple nonsense to presume that Ford Motor Company acted on its own or that it was merely the market's invisible hand at work.[23]

One final story line also deserves attention. Here again, first-class history would help. When homes are flooded, when crops are destroyed by drought, and when shifting sands and sliding hillsides crack foundations, our cultural tendency is to blame nature. Natural disasters, we call them—acts of God. When a river fails to provide enough water to drink, it is apparently the river's fault, or so our rhetoric presumes.

How different our stories would be if we put the blame where it typically belongs, not on the gusty winds but on the three little pigs that failed to build a sturdy house. When homes are built in a floodplain, the flood damage realistically is caused by the home-builder, not nature. (The homebuilder might properly share blame with landowners upstream, whose drains and levees exacerbated the problem.) When crops wither in semiarid lands, it is mostly the result of a farmer taking a land-use gamble. Concrete foundations have no place on unstable soils. When tilled hillsides wash away in the heavy rain, surely it is the tiller's fault, not the rainmaker's.[24]

These six elements are the lead intellectual challenges that the conservation cause now faces. They are as important, if not more so, than the particular problems now being addressed. Good resolutions of them would aid efforts to deal with the full range of environmental ills.

One missing element remains to be taken up, and that is the desirability of linking the work of conservation to America's evolving story of itself: to our nation's explanation of where we have been, where we are heading, and what we are now called to do.

It is a trite complaint that modern culture exalts the individual self and equates the good life with material gratification. The criticism is overdrawn; if everyone were self-indulgent, the conservation cause would have withered. Still, the lament has substance. It provides both a frustration and an opportunity for conservationists looking ahead.

It is a frustration because only the sensitive few really link their personal happiness with a life that sustains good land in an ecological sense. It is an opportunity because far more people yearn to feel that their lives are woven into a narrative larger and more important than themselves. People long for a sense that they are participants in a sweeping, morally charged experiment. New England Puritans and other settlers sensed their participation in a vital religious mission, structured by God and guided by his hand. They were called to align their lives with God's firm instruction, for their own welfare and the world's salvation. That sense of mission diminished over time, yet it remains alive among many people today. It wells up in the resurgence of evangelical Christianity and other religious movements.

For a good many Americans, it is essential that the Universe contain or fit within a moral order, one that includes them and situates them, along with other faithful people, in an exalted if demanding position.[25] Creationism is one sign of this yearning. So are a number of other fundamentalist religious beliefs. What many critics of the creationist impulse fail to see is that creationism is not chiefly about opposing science. It is about a widely felt discomfort with a view of the world as nothing more than physical substance, devoid of moral value. Is the world meaningless or meaningful in a moral sense? Is it just physical stuff, cleverly arranged, or is there some inherent meaning and value embedded with it? That is the issue on which creationists weigh in so passionately. And it is a fair and legitimate question. Between the two options, which view of things is more likely to produce respect toward nature? Should we view nature as merely atoms, bumping around complexly with no intrinsic value or meaning whatsoever, or should we view it as something more and other than that? Before answering, we might keep in mind that science places humans at the same amoral level as rocks. From the perspective of natural and physical scientists, humans and rocks are just so much physical stuff. The idea that humans possess moral value is entirely a product of human convention. Indeed, the claim that humans possess natural rights has exactly as much scientific support as does the claim that God has guided all evolution. According to environmental historians, science's purely mechanistic view of the planet has aided and abetted our abuse of it. When nature is just physical stuff, valuable only insofar as we want it to be valuable, degradation becomes easy.

By the early years of the nineteenth century, America's sense of religious mission had faded considerably. Its decline left room for the emergence of a new sense of national mission, one linked to the nation's role in promoting liberty and democracy worldwide and to its westward continental expansion. Abraham Lincoln gave this new mission its most eloquent voice.[26] The United States, Lincoln told us, was the last, best hope of democracy. It was a claim easy to believe in the mid-nineteenth century, when nearly every European democracy was tumbling under revolt or invasion. America was one of the few democracies still holding on. It was the beckoning home of freedom and opportunity, the place where the world's poor could begin life anew. It was a grand story that Mr. Lincoln had to tell, and it became grander still as the nation gained in wealth and stature. By the beginning of the next century a reoriented, morally charged United States stood ready to cross an ocean and to shed blood to make the world safe—not for Christian salvation, but for liberty and democracy.

This new national story, though, also began to fray at the edges after a time, despite the punctuated victories over totalitarianism near mid-century. The disappointing aftermath of World War I, the Depression, the scares of the 1950s, the turmoil of the 1960s, Vietnam, and Watergate—these and other events all helped bring it down. Given these setbacks and embarrassments, it became harder to feel that our lives were made meaningful simply because we were Americans and lived in our city on a hill, inexorably guiding the world to a freer, better place.

We find ourselves today, as historian Andrew Delbanco has observed, treading water.[27] We await the rise of some new narrative, some new moral order to replace what we have lost. In the meantime, the individual self has gained ascendancy. We labor away mostly to grow our economy and feed the insatiable self. Immediately after the terrorist acts of September 11, President Bush could think of little to say (aside from vows to get tough) other than to encourage Americans to keep shopping. We live smaller lives, Delbanco relates, fearful that we shall die, as we lived, in a morally empty world that took no note of us.[28]

New narratives, though, do not emerge on a blank slate. They build on the old ones that they replace. They rise up by steps, visibly retaining parts of the old, just as Abraham Lincoln's narrative made conspicuous use of biblical references and religious adages. An earlier vision of Christian redemption became, through Lincoln, a new vision of America as redeemer nation.

Faded though it is, our sense of national exceptionalism still lives on, modestly strengthened by the Soviet Union's collapse and by military successes overseas, including crusades to liberate Kuwait and bring democracy to Iraq. When Americans express patriotism, we implicitly assert that we are more and better than citizens of other nations. We Americans do not merely defend ourselves against attack; even trivial nations display patriotism of that garden-variety sort. Our patriotism is different and higher because the

United States is different and higher. It is raised up by a noble purpose: to spread freedom, democracy, and economic opportunity around the globe.

Conservation has had its own narratives of national development, negative ones mostly. They have been tales of declension, involving English-speaking settlers who arrived on a beautiful continent, cut the trees, eroded the soils, polluted the waters, and otherwise degraded the fertile land. A less harsh conservation tale about America's history accepts the propriety of our national enterprise up until industrialism began to take things too far. At that point, sometime around the early twentieth century, perhaps, we shifted from taming the land to abusing it. Our national campaign to settle the land became something else, something more selfish and destructive.

Modern America awaits the emergence of a new moral narrative. A well-composed narrative would draw from the past, with clear reminders of our religious and national senses of purpose. It would attend to our self-understanding as a free people, while displaying memories of frontier days when we labored to carve farms and cities out of the wilderness. A new narrative would look forward more than it looked back, dangling before us a vision of a better future. And it would encourage Americans to do what we have done so well in the past: to serve as model for the rest of the world, a model not of extravagant living (though we have done that) but of justice and morality. It would call us, in short, to continue our exceptional work.

It is hard to imagine an American president standing up and doing for the land what Abraham Lincoln did for the union and for slaves. But it is not out of the question for the conservation community to designate a leader who is looked to for guidance. If the conservation community could collectively address its various intellectual tasks, perhaps it could also elevate one or more public figures, leaders who could attract the public's attention and who, in interviews and speeches, could introduce new rhetoric and a new national narrative. What if the twenty or fifty or (better still) one hundred largest conservation groups in the country formed a working coalition? What if they chose a statesman-leader, and then used their publicity powers to accentuate what the leader had to say, as part of a larger package of conservation messages?

Whether or not such a leader will emerge, it seems instructive to compose a talk for that leader to give: a talk intended not to inform audiences about specific environmental problems but to help situate conservation within America's story of itself. A good many Americans might just listen, for there is a thirst for something more worthy than military operations overseas. Among the audiences for such a talk would be conservation groups themselves. They need help in knowing how best to communicate their work. They, too, need help in understanding what conservation is about.

A Conservation Message to the American People

Our nation was founded over two centuries ago as a land of freedom and opportunity, a beacon to the oppressed of the world. Since then, Americans have played a variety of special roles in the history of the world. We were a political anomaly at birth, the only nation that thought it possible or even desirable to give sovereign power to the people, rather than to a king or aristocracy. By our success we showed that the people could handle this power. And not just handle it, but exercise sovereign power more wisely than could any other political form.

We founded our nation on principles of freedom that gave people unprecedented opportunities. We also strived for, and sometimes achieved, extraordinary levels of justice, while fostering an economic system whose prosperity has been the envy of the world. We've crossed our borders to help people elsewhere overcome tyrants. And we've shed our blood, so that freedom and democracy could grow around the world.

As we've done this, though, we've been mindful of our blessings. High among them has been the blessing of our fertile, productive land. We can credit our farmers with exceptional aptitude and energy, but they'd be the first to admit that nature plays the bigger role. No sooner had the first English settlers stepped ashore in Virginia and Massachusetts than they paused to give thanks for this unearned natural bonanza. The settlers knew just how fortunate they were to arrive in a land where forests and fertile plains spread beyond the horizon.

The North American continent was occupied by native peoples, of course. And our treatment of them too often brought us shame. Indeed, looking back, we are prone to shake our heads at how long it took to widen our senses of community to include native Indians as full-fledged members. But step-by-step we have done that, or tried to. We have taken seriously the lofty principles with which our nation began.

The American continent was a divinely inspired place for these first European settlers, just as it was morally infused for the native Indians. The land was God's Creation, so our ancestors said, and so many of us still say today. One of our strongest duties as a people has been to respect that Creation. We stood as a city upon a hill, with the eyes of the world upon us. Would we tend this land with care? Would we form here a more inclusive, morally guided community? Would we be a place where peace, justice, and prosperity could all reside?

As a people we've made our mistakes, plenty of them. And we've professed commitments to moral standards that we weren't ready to fulfill. Still, we've been mature enough to admit our errors and strong enough to keep striving. When we've had to, we've made great sacrifices. We've tightened our belts and gone without. We've shed our blood, lots of it, not just to protect our prosperity but to stand up for our principles. A pioneering, can-do spirit runs in our veins.

Over the generations our population has risen and our technological prowess has expanded, so much so that we've found ourselves, many times, pushing nature too hard. We have cut into the land's principal, and not just lived off the income. We've driven away too many wild species, drained too many rivers, and disrupted natural processes that keep the land fertile. The truth is, we've been harvesting more than the land produces, year by year. We've been drawing down our bank balance with nature. Today we face a new challenge, to find ways to *keep* the land healthy, to maintain the land's fertility, diversity, and beauty. And to accomplish this not for one generation but for many.

This new challenge is one that we cannot ignore. It is no less important than any that we have faced in the past. To meet it, we'll need to adjust our world-leading civilization so that we take better care of the nature around us. The land is our home, this grand Creation. We occupy it together, often close together. As our scientists remind us regularly, nature is an intricate, interconnected web of life. What we do to nature in one place can have ripple effects that show up far away. The health and happiness of one family is linked to the activities of neighbors, both near and far.

The time has come to make our landscapes, our homes, as healthy, beautiful, and pleasing as they can be. This is one of the tasks of our time. We need to elevate the quality and health of our lands and of our lives, not just the quantity of our belongings.

Benjamin Franklin put the point this way to his fellow Revolutionaries: we either hang together, or we shall all hang separately. The Revolutionaries were in it together, and so are we today. The social fabric of our nation forms an interwoven whole. Injustice to one of us is injustice to our collective whole. So, too, with our lands, our neighborhoods, our communities, and our wild places. Ill health in one place means ill health in the home that we all inhabit.

When the world looks to the United States today—holding us to high standards, as it has and should—a number of questions are being implicitly asked. Having achieved this great prosperity, can America now *maintain* it? Can we live prosperously without degrading our soils, without fouling our waters and air, and without diminishing our vast biological riches? Can this world-leading nation feed, clothe, and shelter its people, all of them, without slowly degrading the fertile continent that it occupies?

Good questions, all of them. Yet, if we remember where we have been as a nation and what our predecessors accomplished over the past four centuries, the answers should be plain. Yes, we can rise to these challenges. We can indeed show the world that prosperity and healthy lands can go hand in hand. We can indeed demonstrate that freedom, private property, and individual initiative can all be sustained, even as we work collectively to make our homeland healthier, more beautiful, and more supportive of good life. We share our land with one another and with an incredibly diverse array of other life forms. In an important sense we do not own it. We are merely stewards and tenants of it. We shoulder a duty to care for nature for the benefit of our grandchildren and their grandchildren.

What I've been talking about is a new kind of progress, a new, broader vision of community, one that includes all life and future generations. America at its founding represented what was then a new kind of progress in terms of individual human rights. Since then, we've revised and expanded our definition of progress, generation by generation. We've also expanded the boundaries of our communities, reaching out and drawing in new members, peoples of different colors and backgrounds and languages. What I am talking about now is a continuation of this world-respected work. I am talking about changing our ways of living on the land—our farms, forests, pastures, towns, deserts, mountains, suburbs, cities—so that we respect the fundamental, creative forces of nature.

Some among us would ask: Haven't we done enough already? We've made progress in addressing our environmental ills. Can't we declare victory and get on with the business of living?

Our answer, I believe, should be this. Yes, we have made progress, but not enough. We've had successes, but there's more to be done. We need to press on, so that our air everywhere is clean and our waters are clear and free flowing. We need to do more to protect our wildlife and biological communities. Wild creatures are not just sources of joy and instruction. They help sustain the land's health and productivity, in ways that we are still trying to unravel. Our major rivers aren't just highways for ships and barges, they are vital parts of nature's fabric, essential to the health of landscapes. And then we have the soil itself, the foundation of all life on land, as farmers and gardeners well know. Even small soil losses and invisible forms of degradation can mount up over time. We need to gain our daily bread in ways that make the soil better, not worse.

Some among us again would ask: What about our individual liberties, what about our private property rights? Won't these be at risk if we really get serious about promoting land health?

If we do our work right, they will not be at risk. If we each do our fair share, if we each refrain from causing harm, the burdens will be spread among us evenly, right along with the many, many benefits that come from healthy, beautiful lands. Freedom doesn't mean license or profligate living, and it never has. We know that. Freedom in America has meant a responsible kind of individualism. Land ownership, too, is about responsibility. It doesn't include the right to degrade the Earth or to drag down the health and beauty of surrounding lands. Responsibility is the key. Being a good citizen, a good community member, a responsible landowner is the key. We've known this for a long time.

What lies ahead for us, then, is a chance to continue our successful settlement of this continent, by making our homes, farms, forests, and cities all more healthy and habitable. We need to do this not just for future generations but, frankly, for ourselves, so that our own lives can be better. We don't need to look to outer space for challenges. We have them right here at home. They are in the forests and mountains, on the plains and deserts, in our suburbs and cities, and along the rivers and shores that make up our shared inheritance. And we are poised to meet them.

Conservation's Central
Readings

A BIBLIOGRAPHIC ESSAY

For those who want to take conservation seriously, there is no substitute for digging into the leading writings of our most important voices. For some years I have taught to graduate students from various disciplines a readings course on conservation thought, considered as a critique and proposed reformation of modern culture. My suggestions here draw on experiences with the many readings used in that course and on student reactions to them. Inevitably, the list reflects my own assessment; other observers would compile different offerings. My recommendations center around twelve key works, starting with the most important. I offer comments about each work's value and add references to selected similar works.

1. Aldo Leopold, *A Sand County Almanac and Sketches Here and There* (New York: Oxford University Press, 1949). Leopold's classic is the most probing, wide-ranging work on the subject of conservation. In length it is short; in wisdom it overflows. A virtue and drawback of the work is that the words flow so smoothly and the stories are so engaging in narrative terms that it is easy for readers to underestimate the complexity of Leopold's ideas and feelings. First-time readers, having heard of the book's importance, frequently come away from it underwhelmed. The book deserves—and amply repays—multiple careful readings. Leopold was not one to waste words.

To properly understand this work we need to recognize Leopold's chief aim in writing it: not to entertain or to inform, although those goals fit into the mix, but to fundamentally change the reader. Leopold speaks directly to the individual reader, one to one. His hope—implicitly conveyed in the opening essay, "January Thaw"—is that the reader, like the hibernating skunk in his tale, might awaken from slumber and see the land anew, appreciating its details, following up its mysteries, and contemplating the many ways that humans and other animals are alike. By late in life Leopold concluded that conservation required fundamental shifts in the ways people perceived nature and valued it. They needed new aesthetic standards, an enlarged sense of morality, broader senses of community, and more. Leopold's *Almanac,* as a result, operates at various levels. Many readers find it useful to read the book through once with care, grappling with the issues posed in the final essays, and then to go back through the text to see how Leopold works on and with those same issues throughout each essay. "Show, don't tell" was one of Leopold's writing guidelines. Infect readers with your own love of nature; let them see the land through your eyes.

Best known among the *Almanac*'s many pieces is the ultimate one, "The Land Ethic." Leopold wrote it not long before he died, and he doubtless would have revised it before publication, given the chance. (Leopold died one week after the book was accepted for publication; it came out eighteen months later.) "The Land Ethic," in truth, contains far too many ideas in a form too condensed for any ordinary reader to assimilate easily. In its compactness and need for careful parsing, it draws comparison with tight religious texts. To understand the final essay, it is helpful to outline it carefully, identifying the steps in Leopold's argument, and then to delve into each step one by one. It is interesting to note that Leopold intended to have "The Land Ethic" appear first in the book's final section, "The Upshot," not last (the decision to shift it was made by his son, Luna, and Oxford's editors). To read the final four essays in their intended order is to gain a different sense of emphasis. With "The Land Ethic" first in "The Upshot," we see it not as the ultimate answer but more as a point of beginning for serious inquiry, which the three following essays then pursue. Because of its title, many readers plow through the essay until they find the section describing the land ethic, as if all else were mere background. It is easy to pass by, or at least underestimate, Leopold's comments about what conservation should be trying to achieve—the promotion of land health. With "The Land Ethic" first, we end the book with "Wilderness" and with his prophetic pronouncement that "all history consists of successive excursions from a single starting-point, to which man returns again and again to organize yet another search for a durable scale of values." Just such a search, just such a new beginning, was what Leopold thought necessary.

Another good entry point into the *Almanac* is to track down Leopold's original longer foreword. Responding to an editor's suggestion, Leopold wisely provided the much shorter foreword that the book now contains. The original foreword appears in J. Baird Callicott, *A Companion to "A Sand County Almanac"* (Madison: University of Wisconsin Press, 1987), and variations on the longer foreword are found in Leopold's papers, held at the University of Wisconsin Archives in Madison. In it, Leopold comments on many of the book's individual essays, linking them loosely to events in his life and to his own evolving thought. In his typically understated way, he tells us which pieces are most important. He particularly emphasizes the easily overlooked piece "Odyssey," in which he probes what was for him the key land function (maintaining soil fertility) and the central way that humans were degrading land (by shortening food chains and disrupting the land's ability to recycle nutrients). It is hard to overstate the importance of the ideas in "Odyssey" to Leopold's mature conservation thought.

Leading Leopold scholars Susan L. Flader and J. Baird Callicott, in *"The River of the Mother of God" and Other Essays by Aldo Leopold* (Madison: University of Wisconsin Press, 1991), have put together an excellent one-volume sampler, chronologically arranged, of some of Leopold's hundreds of shorter writings. The editors' introduction provides a valuable overview, and the book ends with the best available Leopold bibliography. A shorter collection, focused on Leopold's farmland-related conservation writings and including key essays on land health, is J. Baird Callicott and Eric T. Freyfogle, eds., *For the Health of the Land: Previously Unpublished Essays and Other Writings* (Washington, D.C.: Island Press, 1999). Another book, a collection of Leopold pieces (mostly journal entries describing hunting trips) published soon after his death, is useful chiefly because of the insights it offers on his early career and personal life: Luna B. Leopold, ed., *Round River: From the Journals of Aldo Leopold* (New York: Oxford University Press, 1953). An Oxford cloth and Ballantine paper edition, carrying the title *"A Sand County Almanac" and Other Essays on Conservation from "Round River"* (first published 1966), includes all of Leopold's *Almanac* as well as selections (some condensed) from *Round River*.

Leopold is the subject of an excellent biography, Curt Meine, *Aldo Leopold: His Life and Work* (Madison: University of Wisconsin Press, 1988). His emerging ecological thought is considered in Susan L. Flader, *Thinking Like a Mountain: Aldo Leopold and the Evolution of an Ecological Attitude toward Deer, Wolves, and Forests* (Columbia: University of Missouri Press, 1974). Callicott's valuable essays on Leopold appear in two volumes of his collected works: *In Defense of the Land Ethic: Essays in Environmental Philosophy* (Albany: State University of New York Press, 1989), and *Beyond the Land Ethic: More Essays in Environmental Philosophy* (Albany: State University of New York Press, 1999). Many of Curt Meine's essays appear in *Correction Lines: Essays on Land, Leopold, and Conservation* (Washington, D.C.: Island Press, 2004).

Even with this secondary writing, there is much about Leopold's thought that is poorly understood. His perceptive ideas on conservation economics and private lands conservation, for instance, have received nothing like the attention they deserve. The vast scholarly gaps on his overall goal of land health and on Leopold as cultural reformer have been ably addressed by Julianne Lutz Newton, "The Commonweal of Life: Aldo Leopold and Land Health" (Ph.D. diss., University of Illinois at Urbana-Champaign, 2004; forthcoming from Island Press in 2006). Newton has investigated more thoroughly than anyone the science behind Leopold's ethic and his idea of land health, showing the major ways in which he borrowed from others. She also probes the major nonscience influences on his thinking. In all, her work is both the culmination of a half century of Leopold scholarship and a major point of beginning for further study, particularly on Leopold's cultural criticisms and his belief that conservation required major social change.

2. Wendell Berry, *The Unsettling of America: Culture and Agriculture* (San Francisco: Sierra Club Books, 1977). Berry's work evokes widely differing responses among readers. Many are put off by the circumstances and choices of his life—he runs a small, hilly farm using draft horses rather than a tractor. They assume he is merely calling us to look backward, nostalgically, to some preindustrial era that is long gone, if it ever existed. For others, he is our supreme moralist, a true prophet who sees more clearly than anyone our cultural flaws and who variously encourages, cajoles,

induces, and enjoins us to amend our ways. Berry is easily the most prolific writer on nature and culture at work today, with some forty books to his credit, including half a dozen novels and numerous collections of essays, poems, and short stories. He is a major conservation voice of the era, if not the most important one. Nearly all of his books are in print.

Berry's work is wide-ranging and complex, posing a challenge for those seeking a place to enter. *The Unsettling of America* is perhaps his best-known individual book. It is a hard-hitting critique of the force that has wrought more change to our landscapes than any other: industrial agriculture. The flaws that he finds within agribusiness are more cultural than they are technological, and they appear, he tells us, throughout contemporary society. Berry's style here and in many of his essays is pointed and polemical; he speaks in a strident tone that many readers find harsh and overconfident. Elsewhere, he is more ruminative, reserved, uncertain, and at times refreshingly humorous. In nearly all writings he draws upon the experiences of his own life and those of family and friends. The confidence and harsh judgment that Berry so often displays in his nonfiction is for the most part absent in his masterful novels and stories, all set in a fictionalized version of the region along the Kentucky River (Port Royal in real life, Port William in the fiction) where Berry's family has lived for generations. In Berry's fiction, one sees in action the same challenges, stresses, cultural impulses, moral dilemmas, and human foibles that weave throughout all of his work.

In my graduate course I typically use two of Berry's shortest volumes: a story collection, *The Wild Birds: Six Stories of the Port William Membership* (San Francisco: North Point Press, 1986) and an essay collection, *Another Turn of the Crank* (Washington, D.C.: Counterpoint Press, 1995). In *The Wild Birds* Berry offers narrative variations on the themes of membership, community, and belonging as lived by and among Port William's residents, who vary from the responsible to the deviant. The traits and struggles of the model community member are presented here in the character of Mat Feltner, with lawyer Wheeler Catlett as his worthy if sometimes reluctant successor. Underlying every tale are senses of connection: between people and land, among family members and neighbors, and across the generations. *Another Turn of the Crank* includes some of Berry's most valuable meditations on health, property, nature, and the common good; it provides a solid introduction to his conservation thought.

Berry's short stories are now collected into a single volume, *That Distant Land* (Washington, D.C.: Shoemaker and Hoard, 2004). The book includes features that will delight Berry admirers: a map of the fictional Port William setting and a genealogical chart showing the familial links among the main characters over the 140-year-period covered in his fiction. The stories appear in the order of the time periods in which they are set. Interspersed among entries in the table of contents are the titles of his novels and the years in which they are set. It is thus possible for a devoted reader to proceed easily through all of his fiction in rough order of fictional chronology.

Berry's two longest novels are masterpieces. The earlier one, *A Place on Earth,* rev. ed. (San Francisco: North Point Press, 1983; original longer edition, New York: Harcourt, Brace and World, 1967), is set in the final year of World War II and centers around the Feltner family's recognition that their son Virgil, heir to the agrarian tradition—and, by implication, symbol of the prewar world—will not return from the outburst of industrial destruction then taking place in Europe. The more recent one, *Jayber Crow* (Washington, D.C.: Counterpoint Press, 2000), is Berry's most overtly religious book. The title character struggles to live a virtuous life in spite of the passions within him and the powerful forces that are dragging down his small town and native agrarian culture. Is it possible, Berry asks, to follow the Christian admonition to love one's neighbor when the neighbor's ways of living are bringing ruin to all that one values?

Many of Berry's agrarian essays are collected in Norman Wirzba, ed., *The Art of the Commonplace: The Agrarian Essays of Wendell Berry* (Washington, D.C.: Shoemaker and Hoard, 2002). Agrarianism, the conservation strand of which Berry is the acknowledged leader, is surveyed in two similarly titled collections of writings by leading practitioners and advocates: Eric T. Freyfogle, ed., *The New Agrarianism: Land, Culture, and the Community of Life* (Washington, D.C.: Island Press, 2001); and Norman Wirzba, ed., *The Essential Agrarian Reader: The Future of Culture, Community, and the Land* (Lexington: University Press of Kentucky, 2003). Of the secondary writing on Berry (of which there is little that takes him seriously as a conservation figure), the best is Kimberly K. Smith, *Wendell Berry and the Agrarian Tradition: A Common Grace* (Lawrence: University Press of Kansas, 2003). A good literary study that approaches Berry through the various personas he employs is Janet Goodrich, *The Unforeseen Self in the Works of Wendell Berry* (Columbia: University of Missouri Press, 2001).

Throughout his writing Berry makes use of the literary technique of synecdoche, drawing upon the specific example and circumstances of his life to illustrate larger principles and claims. His skilled use of the technique helps make his writing vivid, exact, and appealing. It also accounts, though, for his dismissal by readers who assume that he is offering his own life as the one and true way to dwell. The truth is quite to the contrary. His life and community, Berry tells us, are a microcosm of the larger world, riven by the same tensions and challenges that are at work pretty much everywhere. If his life differs in outward details, it is much the same as all other American lives in the forces that press upon him and upon his natural home. To look beyond his particular case is to reap the intellectual harvest that Berry offers in abundance.

3. Donald Worster, *The Wealth of Nature: Environmental History and the Ecological Imagination* (New York: Oxford University Press, 1993). Like Leopold's classic, Worster's magnificent essay collection is not so much a book as an entire library pressed between two covers. No academic discipline better situates a scholar to see the big picture than history, and Worster is a master of the craft. He takes in the full sweep of America's story, paying particular attention to the ways we have shaped nature and in turn been shaped by it. Although the land appears prominently in every essay, American culture is Worster's target, and his critical observations dig deep. Some essays introduce environmental history and its chief findings while chiding the American history profession generally for underappreciating the vital influences of nature-culture interactions. Other essays attend to our dominant form of land use, farming: what it has done to the land, what it says about us, and how it needs to change. Many essays address water use, particularly the ethos, practices, and social implications of large-scale irrigation. Finest of all, though, are Worster's wide-ranging meditations: on private land, on soil, on environmentalism and religious fervor, on Leopold and Muir, and on our need

collectively to develop modes of living that can last. A penetrating essay critiques the idea of sustainable development; another probes the ways that scientific ideas about ecology have been influenced by prevailing social and political values. Worthy of repeated readings are his explorations of the cultural origins of our environmental predicament, especially the concluding title essay, which plays on Adam Smith's classic work, *The Wealth of Nations.*

Perhaps an easier place to enter Worster's work is his award-winning study, *Dust Bowl: The Southern Plains in the 1930s* (New York: Oxford University Press, 1979). Better than any other occurrence in our history, the Dust Bowl brought into sharp relief the strengths and weaknesses of our culture: our entrepreneurial energy and commitment to individual initiative, and our denial of nature's limits and our unwillingness to shape our lives to the land. Worster probes the cultural and natural reasons why the Dust Bowl occurred, recounts the ways the catastrophe was interpreted and how the public responded to it, and explains why much-needed major reform measures largely failed. The Dust Bowl offered opportunities for us to learn. By and large, we ignored them. To understand what we could have learned, and why we failed to do so, is to gain great insight into the challenges facing conservation today.

The serious student will want to take in Worster's penetrating study of the cultural contexts of ecological thought, *Nature's Economy: A History of Ecological Ideas,* 2nd ed. (Cambridge: Cambridge University Press, 1994). Also good is *Rivers of Empire: Water, Aridity, and the Growth of the American West* (New York: Pantheon Books, 1986). There, Worster meditates on the ways that the control of water in arid places has led to, and helped solidify, hierarchical societies of unequal wealth; the control of nature too often has meant the control of some people by other people, with nature as the tool. Worster's essays dealing with culture in the American West and the particular difficulties we have had adjusting to its natural harshness appear in *Under Western Skies: Nature and History in the American West* (New York: Oxford University Press, 1992). More recently Worster has turned to biographies. *A River Running West: The Life of John Wesley Powell* (New York: Oxford University Press, 2001) and a forthcoming biography of John Muir.

Worster has written little directly about the conservation movement itself. Studies by other historians vary greatly in quality. The most reliable observer is historian Samuel P. Hays, whose chief works on the past half century are *Beauty, Health, and Permanence: Environmental Politics in the United States, 1955–1985* (Cambridge: Cambridge University Press, 1987); *Explorations in Environmental History* (Pittsburgh: University of Pittsburgh Press, 1998); and *A History of Environmental Politics since 1945* (Pittsburgh: University of Pittsburgh Press, 2000).

Readers interested in history would do well to read far beyond these works, for the literature is vast and insightful. In understanding our current cultural plight, environmental history is probably our most valuable academic discipline. A good one-volume introduction to the larger story about Americans and land is Ted Steinberg, *Down to Earth: Nature's Role in American History* (New York: Oxford University Press, 2002). In Steinberg's view, the main cultural idea driving environmental change, for good and ill, has been our tendency to fragment nature and to view its parts as marketable commodities.

4. David Ehrenfeld, *The Arrogance of Humanism* (New York: Oxford University Press, 1981). Admirers of Ehrenfeld's classic work may not be huge in number but they are often intense in their appreciation. Ehrenfeld's broad interests and unusual academic background have helped him view the human experience on Earth in all its physical, moral, and spiritual complexity. Holder of an M.D. degree and a Ph.D. in biology and well read in theological literature (among other fields), he encompasses a wide range indeed. Ehrenfeld traces our conservation challenges to the Enlightenment Era of the seventeenth and eighteenth centuries, when empirical data collection, human reason, and a human-centered view of the world gained dominance. We are less powerful than we think we are, Ehrenfeld tells us; reason is a wonderful tool, but we are prone to

exaggerate what it can do; our technology is impressive but it has not solved, and cannot solve, all the problems that we are causing.

No true conservation can occur, Ehrenfeld claims, so long as we approach our problems strictly in terms of human needs and if we make judgments that rely solely on our senses and rational faculties. As do conservation's other leading voices, Ehrenfeld urges us to enhance and make greater use of our moral and spiritual faculties. He ends his book with specific suggestions: We need to reduce our arrogance and endeavor to shape our lives to nature's ways; we need to stop assuming that all problems are solvable by human reason and new technology. Ehrenfeld's volume is particularly valuable for its comprehensive look at the values that justify species conservation (Ehrenfeld, a sea turtle researcher, was founding editor of the journal *Conservation Biology* as well as a longtime contributor to the journal *Orion*). In the end, concludes Ehrenfeld, we can argue for the protection of all life forms only based on aesthetics and morality; even a broadly defined assessment of human needs cannot get us there.

Ehrenfeld's more recent books build on this base and offer penetrating observations on the events of our time: *Beginning Again: People and Nature in the New Millennium* (New York: Oxford University Press, 1993) and *Swimming Lessons: Keeping Afloat in the Age of Technology* (New York: Oxford University Press, 2002). They are made up mostly of essays, all well crafted, that first appeared in a periodical. Taken as a whole, his powerful body of work offers nothing less than a blueprint for a fundamental shift in the direction the Western world has taken over the past three centuries.

Also useful is a finely written presentation of "ecologism" (as the author terms it) as a coherent alternative to the dominant American culture: Charles Sokol Bednar, *Transforming the Dream: Ecologism and the Shaping of an Alternative American Vision* (Albany: State University of New York Press, 2003). This alternative cultural perspective toward nature has no home on the political spectrum. In *Mindful Conservatism: Rethinking the Ideological and Educational Basis of an Ecologically Sustainable Future* (Lanham, Md.: Rowman and Littlefield, 2003), C. A. Bowers offers a penetrating critique of current political uses of the term *conservatism.* He offers a thoughtful plea for a perspective that he labels "mindful conservatism" and considers the changes that could be made in education to implement it.

5. Rachel Carson, *Silent Spring* (New York: Houghton Mifflin, 1962). Carson's extraordinarily influential book is commonly thought of as a study of pesticides and their ill effects. It is such a study, as best she could undertake it at the time, under hostile circumstances and with the limited knowledge then available. But it is far more than that, and to focus only on the pesticide details is to miss its enduring

value. When Carson wrote her work she was a well-known, best-selling author of science books about the sea and seashores. For years she had gathered information about the dangers of pesticides and the ecological implications of their widespread use. What most alarmed her, though, was the fact that the pesticides were being used with so little thought, with so little public disclosure, and with no attempt to obtain the consent of people affected by them. The larger problem, then, had to do with politics, power, the erosion of democracy, and the invasion of individual rights.

Much serious conservation writing embeds humans into larger ecological orders and speaks to the overall health or condition of that larger order. Carson was supremely ecological in her attentiveness to the ripple effects of tugging at nature in one place. Yet at the same time, she was a strong believer in the dignity and integrity of the individual human standing alone and in the fundamental political principles on which our nation was founded. All of these, she concluded, were endangered by the nation's pesticide-use program. Government had largely been taken over by powerful commercial interests. The public had little say in fundamental decisions affecting their lands and lives. Caution was being thrown to the wind. Alternative approaches to pest prevention (what today is termed integrated pest management) were largely ignored in the name of corporate gain, despite considerable evidence of their effectiveness. Pesticides were being spread on people's farms, yards, ponds, houses, even directly on their bodies, without so much as telling them what the dangers were and asking their consent. In her subsequent testimony to Congress, she posed the issue starkly. Widespread pesticide use abridged the fundamental, constitutionally protected liberties of the American people. It violated our individual rights.

Carson's work today stands as the preeminent expression of this individual-rights perspective on environmental issues. Carson had one foot in community ecology and the other in America's liberal tradition and its respect for individual integrity. As well as anyone she spoke of the need to exercise caution and to use sensible burdens of proof. Barely concealed was her outrage at how government had been abusing the public trust. Between the lines she diagnosed the problem—our cultural infatuation with science, our adoration of big business, our near single-minded utilitarian commitment to wealth creation, and our willingness to use immediate human utility to judge the rightness or wrongness of our acts. Her book is a testimony to the power of one person to effect change. It is usefully considered, too, as a damning critique of American culture and the political order. Where Ehrenfeld would later speak about general principles and tease out the precise cultural assumptions that required change, Carson did the same, just as powerfully, by showing how our arrogance had brought on massive death.

Carson's best-selling nature books remain wonderful reading. Her editor at Houghton Mifflin, Paul Brooks, has pieced together an unusual book by and about Carson that offers an engaging introduction to her professional work. His *The House of Life: Rachel Carson at Work* (New York: Houghton Mifflin, 1972; reprinted in 1989 by Sierra Club Books as *Rachel Carson: The Writer at Work*) weaves the story of her life around lengthy excerpts from her major books.

6. Edward Abbey, *Desert Solitaire: A Season in the Wilderness* (New York: McGraw Hill, 1968). A decade and a half after his death, Abbey remains the intellectual leader of the more radical strand of the environmental movement. Although he was not an ecoterrorist himself and did not particularly endorse it (though he expressed sympathy with the impulse), his fierce commitment to wild places and wild things, and his willingness to lash out like a cornered animal at those who were despoiling his natural home, encouraged many readers to undertake direct action. Abbey's popular novel, *The Monkey Wrench Gang* (New York: J. B. Lippincott, 1975), gave the ecoterrorist effort its all-purpose verb: monkey wrenching. So critical was Abbey of American culture that he saw little reason for hope. He expected the system to crash, and he tried to look ahead, particularly in his fiction, to what life would be like amid the rubble as the still-living remnant attempted to start life anew.

Desert Solitaire is Abbey's most enduring work. Its title invites many comparisons, particularly to the early Christian founders of desert monasticism and to the forty-day pilgrimage of Jesus himself before he began his public ministry. Despite the subtitle, Abbey's visit to the wilderness (mostly the Utah desert) took place over several years (in condensing the story to a single season, he followed the lead of Thoreau in *Walden*). Like spiritual pilgrims before him, Abbey went to immerse himself in his surroundings. What he encountered, though, was not a land infused with spirits and loaded with hidden romantic messages about how we ought to live. Instead, he found a natural world that was inscrutable and completely disinterested in human life: a hostile, haunting, terrifying, supremely beautiful land that humans could either adapt to or die. Like Thoreau and (even more) John Muir, Abbey craved for direct experience with nature, and he got it. He admired greatly the life forms that could thrive in the hostile environment of the desert. "The singleleaf ash in my garden stands alone along the path, a dwarf tree only three feet high but tough and enduring, clenched to the stone." And thus Abbey himself: clenched to the big stone of the arid and mountainous West and intending to hold on with just as much toughness and tenacity.

Abbey's book includes many of the messages that surface in other conservation writings about the vastness of human ignorance, our cultural decadence, our need to bend our ways to those of nature, and others.

What stands out here so starkly is the sense of wildness and wild things as essential sources of life and vitality, for humans as well as other species. Much of our cultural decay, Abbey tells us, has come about precisely because we have become so detached from the wilds. We have become like so many domesticated animals: fat, slow, stupid, and utterly unable to look after ourselves without massive help. Abbey's conservation ethic is usefully compared with that of Rachel Carson, despite their widely differing personal lives. Like Carson, Abbey boiled things down to the individual level—to himself, usually. His sense of liberty was strong, and he defined it broadly. Liberty was not just about keeping government off our backs. It was about the freedom of one man to live openly without interference from neighbors; it was about the ability to drink water from a creek without being contaminated by industrial and agribusiness pollutants. Bring back the predators, Abbey yelled. Get out of the car, grab a canteen, and head out to the wilds, before you go crazy.

Desert Solitaire is a carefully orchestrated drama that may or may not have much connection to events that actually happened to Abbey during his Utah years. It is laced with Old Testament references and with stark images and colorful characters, human and animal. In an early chapter, "The Serpents of Paradise," he adds one of his many personal touches: two snakes, rather than one. "The snake story," he tells us, "is not yet ended."

Abbey's many books are all worth reading, although his essays vary in quality. His autobiographical novel, written late in his life and published posthumously, *The Fool's Progress: An Honest Novel* (New York: Henry Holt, 1990), is the work of a masterful storyteller at the height of his form. Here as elsewhere Abbey shows his impatience with mere reform environmentalism that attends to little problems without addressing the big ones. Abbey famously would throw empty beer cans out the truck window rather than recycle them. Why bother, he implicitly asked, if we lack the courage to confront the industrial juggernaut?

An especially literate, passionate expression of the radical environmental "sentiment" is Chrisopher Manes, *Green Rage: Radical Environmentalism and the Unmaking of Civilization* (Boston: Little Brown, 1990), itself a conservation classic.

7. Bryan G. Norton, *Toward Unity among Environmentalists* (New York: Oxford University Press, 1991). If one has time to read only a single book on environmental philosophy, this should be it. Like the best of philosophers, Norton has read widely in environmental literature—and it shows. In this book, Norton perceptively reviews the main strands of philosophical thinking about humans and nature. He then applies the ideas to the major categories of conservation challenges. As readers we sense that we are being led through the fog by someone who

understands the ground thoroughly, who carries a powerful light, and who knows just where to shine it so that we can see where we are. In Norton's view, the intellectual lay of the land is fragmented mostly because of the differing value presumptions that people bring with them when they engage in policy debates about nature. His aim, which he succeeds in achieving, is "to challenge the suggestion that environmentalists hold no common ground, and the associated suggestion that environmentalists represent at best a shifting coalition of interest groups." Norton's refreshing desire, in short, is not to point out how all other philosophers have things wrong and he has them right, or to take something already complex and make it even more so. It is to simplify, to bring together, to make ideas accessible and useable, and to help in the great work of healing the land and its people. Norton urges all of us who consider ourselves conservationists or environmentalists to focus on what we are trying to accomplish and then get together and do it. We shouldn't get bogged down arguing about the details of our value schemes or about the precise reasons why we want to achieve our goals. Too often environmentalists cannot get beyond their disputes over values and explanations, even when they largely agree on the actions they want to support.

Norton is a forceful advocate for a philosophical value scheme that emphasizes the ethical links among generations more so than ethical obligations that humans might have to nature directly. He is not, that is, merely a moral relativist who can get up in the morning, look in the closet, and don whatever ethical garb seems appropriate for the day. Ideas count for him, a great deal, and they are by no means all equally sound. Still, he is passionate in wanting to see the land regain health in ways that make it a good home for people. We need to get on with that work, he tells us, even as we keep thinking and arguing about values and aspirations.

Norton's other works are also filled with wisdom, though none is quite so accessible to the general reader. They include *Why Preserve Natural Variety?* (Princeton: Princeton University Press, 1987) and *Searching for Sustainability: Interdisciplinary Essays in the Philosophy of Conservation Biology* (Cambridge: Cambridge University Press, 2003).

8. David W. Orr, *Earth in Mind: On Education, Environment, and the Human Prospect,* rev. ed. (Washington, D.C.: Island Press, 2004). Orr heads the environmental studies program at Oberlin College. Before then, he and his brother ran an experimental learning center in rural Arkansas. He is passionate about education and just as passionate about reforming it, dramatically and soon. In this collection of brief, jam-packed essays, Orr's fertile mind roams widely through our culture and our chief institutions, finding much that is amiss. He is the son of a preacher, and his

discourses tend to come in sermon-sized bites, loaded with punch. Orr's work is most valuable and most deserving of a high place on any reading list because he has attended particularly to the problems and possibilities of formal schooling, including higher education. He proposes that we turn it inside out, literally, so that we connect students to the local lands and get them to see their fundamental dependence on nature. His call for a core ecological curriculum for all students is ambitious. Equally ambitious has been the architectural design effort that he propelled at Oberlin, which has created one of the most environmentally advanced institutional buildings in the world. The project itself was an educational effort by and for students; the resulting building, Orr proclaims, is an important, continuing part of Oberlin's curriculum, as are the nearby gardens and the advanced waste-treatment capabilities.

Orr's other writings include *Ecological Literacy: Education and the Transition to a Postmodern World* (Albany: State University of New York Press, 1992) and his exploration of the many conservation possibilities that attend the use of nature as design template, *Nature of Design: Ecology, Culture, and Human Intention* (New York: Oxford University Press, 2002). Orr's prose rises to an even sharper, more penetrating level in *The Last Refuge: Patriotism, Politics, and the Environment in an Age of Terror* (Washington, D.C.: Island Press, 2004). Here Orr lashes our sagging civic culture. He calls for a revitalization of our senses of citizenship, patriotism, and democratic rule. As does Wendell Berry, Orr traces much of our confusion to our sloppiness in using words, particularly those that describe our political life and public choices. ("By some strange alchemy, the word 'conservative' has been co-opted by those intending to conserve nothing except the rules of the game by which they are greatly enriched.") Echoing Aldo Leopold, he condemns the conservation cause for its fragmentation and inability to act in concert. ("The public, I think, knows what we are against," Orr rails, "but not what we are for.") Recurring messages in his writings are the need to respect connections, to seek systemic and holistic solutions, to honor nature's produce by ensuring that it returns to the land to make new soil.

9. Wes Jackson, *New Roots for Agriculture*, rev. ed. (Lincoln: University of Nebraska Press, 1985). One of the central claims of conservation thought is that people need to bend their ways so as to come into greater alignment with nature, in the process making use of nature's embedded wisdom. No conservation figure has better framed his work around that principle than plant geneticist Wes Jackson, cofounder and head of the Land Institute in Salina, Kansas. Jackson's book is overtly about agriculture and the radically different approach to it that he embraces. Yet, like other conservation masterpieces, the book is far more than

its ostensible subject. Woven into the factual narrative, in a way similar to *Silent Spring,* is Jackson's proposal for a redirection of American culture. Jackson, a first-rate scientific researcher, believes that research can help us find vastly better ways to live on land. At the same time, he is powerfully affected by how little we know and by the benefits we would gain if we acted more humbly and took lessons from species that have been around for millions of years longer than we have. His approach to agriculture, then, is best understood as a design methodology of wide applicability.

Jackson's other books, also brief and to the point (as befits his manner of speech), are every bit as good: *Becoming Native to This Place* (Lexington: University Press of Kentucky, 1994) and *Altars of Unhewn Stone* (San Francisco: North Point Press, 1987), along with a collection coedited with William Vitek, *Rooted in the Land: Essays on Community and Place* (New Haven: Yale University Press, 1996). A more thorough explanation of the research methodology used at the Land Institute is offered in Judith D. Soule and Jon K. Piper, *Farming in Nature's Image: An Ecological Approach to Agriculture* (Washington, D.C.: Island Press, 1992).

10. William Cronon, *Changes in the Land: Indians, Colonists, and the Ecology of New England* (New York: Hill and Wang, 1983). Like Worster, Cronon is one of our leading environmental historians, and just

as Worster moved from an eastern university back to his Kansas homeland, so, too, Cronon gave up a position at Yale to move to the city of his youth, Madison, Wisconsin. Cronon's book long has been a staple of a variety of university courses, including many quite distant from American history; in several law schools, for instance, it is part of the readings in property law. What makes Cronon's study so valuable is the juxtaposition it offers of two radically different orientations toward the same natural landscape (seventeenth-century New England): the approach of the native Indians and that of the incoming English settlers. Cronon recounts how the Indians made use of the lands and the ecological effects of their uses (as best they can be discerned). He then contrasts them with the far different land-use practices employed by the colonists. Along the way we learn what aspects of colonial practice brought the greatest change (domesticated animals, above all). What arises out of this history is far more than just a new installment in the colonial American story. We get an exceptionally clear look at the links between culture and environmental change and thus an enhanced ability to see how nature and culture are complexly and dialectically intertwined. Augmenting Cronon's formal comparison of Indians and colonists is a further comparison brought to bear by the attentive reader: that between the seventeenth century and American society today. History is at its most valuable when it enables us to stand back and look anew at the world in which we live; it is the centerpiece of Cicero's educational aim to enable students to escape the tyranny of the present. In that educational task, Cronon's book is invaluable.

Also valuable is Cronon's *Nature's Metropolis: Chicago and the Great West* (New York: W. W. Norton, 1991), which considers how Chicago's rise to importance was linked to its role as a hub for the flow of diverse natural resources, from the timber in the North to the grains and hogs from the South and West. Cronon's particular comments about ecological degradation caused by colonial land-use patterns should be read along with Brian Donahue's far more detailed study of a particular corner of New England, *The Great Meadow: Farmers and the Land in Colonial Concord* (New Haven: Yale University Press, 2004). Donahue concludes that while colonial settlers altered the land significantly, ecological degradation largely arrived in the nineteenth century under the pressure of social and economic forces that undercut earlier modes of farming.

One reason why Cronon's *Changes in the Land* deserves a place on the list is because of its rare critical look at the institution of private property, American style. Aldo Leopold called for a new understanding of land ownership, but few conservationists since then have grappled seriously with the institution. For many, it appears, property is largely a given: an obstacle on the path that we simply need to deal with as best we can. Cronon's book does not examine American law, but by contrasting the Anglo-American approach to owning land with the far different ownership arrangement of the native Indians, he jars us out of our complacency. Far more serious conservation writing on private property rights in land is needed.

Historian Adam Rome considers the institution of private property in the course of discussing an otherwise overlooked strand of environmentalism in *The Bulldozer in the Countryside: Suburban Sprawl and the Rise of American Environmentalism* (Cambridge: Cambridge University Press, 2001). He tells about the rising (if faint) call for a more ecologically grounded understanding of what it means to own land, particularly ecologically sensitive lands. The issue also appears in historian Brian Donahue's provocative study, *Reclaiming the Commons: Community Farms and Forests in a New England Town* (New Haven: Yale University Press, 1999), which explores the possible ecological and cultural values of working community-run farms and forests as ways to attach people to their surrounding landscapes. I offer comments of my own on the past and possible future of private property as an institution in *The Land We Share: Private Property and the Common Good* (Washington, D.C.: Island Press, 2003).

11. David Quammen, *The Song of the Dodo: Island Biogeography in an Age of Extinctions* (New York:

Scribner, 1996). Any sensible land conservation strategy will include as a central element a call to promote and revive wildlife populations. Wildlife is not just another issue on the conservation agenda; it is perhaps the key issue, both because of its intrinsic and ecological importance and because wildlife can usefully serve as a goal for management aimed at the broader target of healthy, beautiful lands. To understand serious land conservation one needs to understand the biodiversity component, particularly in terms of population dynamics, evolutionary change, and the causes of both speciation and extinction. The subject is complex. Thankfully, one of our most gifted science writers has taken it up—David Quammen—in a highly readable inquiry that pays particular attention to islands, so important in the evolution of planetary life over time. So engaging is Quammen's work that the reader hardly realizes how much science it contains and how widely it roams. Having set forth the biological basics in his engaging stories about islands, Quammen turns inland to show how and why habitat fragmentation on mainlands creates biological conditions similar to those on islands—including the same threats to species survival.

A more nuts-and-bolts book on biodiversity conservation that translates biological principles into land-use applications is Reed F. Noss and Allen Y. Cooperrider, *Saving Nature's Legacy: Protecting and Restoring Biodiversity* (Washington, D.C.: Island Press, 1994). The fact-filled Noss and Cooperrider volume points out in detail what it would take in land-use terms to protect all life on wide geographical scales. The same material is covered in more detail and with many valuable asides in a highly readable text, Gary K. Meffe and C. Ronald Carroll, *Principles of Conservation Biology,* 2nd ed. (Sunderland, Mass.: Sinauer Associates, 1997). These volumes and others set forth the basics of the essential discipline of conservation biology. Even land conservationists who have little connection to wildlife-related work would do well to read these eye-opening books. To see what wildlife conservation would entail in terms of land-use planning is to see how radically we need to rework the mechanisms for making decisions about land.

Biodiversity conservation is the kind of conservation activity that requires coordinated action on large spatial scales. Tract-by-tract work, when not done pursuant to a clear land-use vision, is unlikely to get it done. Indeed, conservation work without a clearly stated goal is not going to bring it about. Particularly in the case of wide-ranging wildlife species, conservation requires collective action across present-day boundaries as well as a new understanding of private landownership that entails an obligation to share land with wild things. All of this is clearly presented in these useful works. David Wilcove, another skilled wildlife scientist, gives us a much-needed status report on American wildlife in *The Condor's Shadow: The Loss and Recovery of Wildlife in America* (New York: W. H. Freeman, 1994).

12. Herman E. Daly and John B. Cobb, *For the Common Good: Redirecting the Economy toward Community, the Environment, and a Sustainable Future*, 2nd ed. (Boston: Beacon Press, 1994). The dominant vocabulary used today to talk about land and resource use is economics, or economic science, as its practitioners sometimes like to call it. Behind the blizzard of numbers and formulas there exists, most people presume, a solid, incontrovertible methodology for assessing how well we are doing, economically speaking, in getting ahead in the world. The truth, though, is quite otherwise, or rather the truthfulness of what economists conclude is dependent (as all conclusions are dependent) on the assumptions that are used in their work. Economists tend to like the market, they like individual liberty, and they embrace a constellation of human-centered, empirically based values and assumptions that conflict directly with important elements of conservation thought. Given the assumptions that they use, it is little wonder that they reach conclusions that many conservationists find misguided. To varying degrees economists realize that the market is technically flawed and needs corrective measures for it to work right (although the extent of needed correction is often understated greatly because of their limited attentiveness to nature). They are less prone, generally speaking, to realize that the market is a highly distorted and distorting lens through which to see the world, nor is there much recognition that

the market solidifies a way of perceiving nature that is itself a cause of degradation. As critics have long said, it is astonishing, for instance, that calculations of gross domestic product ignore the consumption and degradation of nature. Thus, according to economists, when we cut down a tree the wood is pure economic gain; we need not include in our calculations the fact that we no longer have a living tree.

Taking the lead in promoting an economics that takes ecology and ethics into account is economist Herman E. Daly. His chief work, coauthored with theologian John B. Cobb, is a wide-ranging look at some of the flaws of contemporary neoclassical economics seen from the perspective of an insider who knows and cares about the land. The book offers an eye-opening look at how economics could be radically changed in ways that would make conservation appear less costly and more sensible. Many of the presumed costs of conservation arise largely because the measurement methodologies used are so skewed against it; more accurate accounting methods would yield far different conclusions. A more systematic coverage of the subject, with careful attention to the market's flaws in taking care of land, is Herman E. Daly and Joshua Farley, *Ecological Economics: Principles and Applications* (Washington, D.C.: Island Press, 2004). Even readers with little background in economics would benefit from this book, so clear is the writing and so well do the authors succeed in presenting their ideas simply.

The most spirited, penetrating critique of economic growth theory—that is, of the progressive, progrowth religion that largely dominates our culture—has been penned, surprisingly, by an ecologist, Brian Czech, in his *Shoveling Fuel for a Runaway Train: Errant Economists, Shameful Spenders, and a Plan to Stop Them All* (Berkeley: University of California Press, 2000). A useful, easy-to-read introduction to the subject is Eric A. Davidson, *You Can't Eat GNP: Economics as if Ecology Mattered* (Cambridge, Mass.: Perseus, 2000).

Acknowledgments

Chapter 1 began life as a talk delivered at a conference on reconstructing conservation, held at Woodstock, Vermont, in November 2001. It first appeared in different form under the title "Conservation and the Four Faces of Resistance," in Ben Minteer and Robert Manning, eds., *Reconstructing Conservation: History, Values, and Practice* (Washington, D.C.: Island Press, 2003). My thanks go to the editors of that volume and to the participants in the conference for comments on my presentation. Chapter 2 was also first delivered as a talk, at a conference on innovations in environmental policy held in 1999 at the University of Illinois College of Law. It first appeared in different form as "Five Paths of Environmental Scholarship," *University of Illinois Law Review* (2000): 115–34. Finally, a version of chapter 3 initially appeared in the science journal

Conservation Biology (August 2004) under the title "Conservation and the Lure of the Garden." I thank that journal's editor, Gary Meffe; assigning editor Curt Meine; and anonymous reviewers for their help with the piece. Several anonymous reviewers enlisted by Yale University Press made valuable comments on the volume as a whole, and I am grateful to them.

Notes

Introduction

1. The leading history of efforts at the federal level is Samuel P. Hays, *Conservation and the Gospel of Efficiency: The Progressive Conservation Movement, 1890–1920* (New York: Atheneum, 1969). A recent brief assessment is offered in Curt Meine, *Correction Lines: Essays on Land, Leopold, and Conservation* (Washington, D.C.: Island Press, 2004), 13–35, 42–63. The many sources that consider conservation efforts at local levels, which were often motivated by desires to protect ways of life tied to nature, include John T. Cumbler, *Reasonable Use: The People, the Environment, and the State, New England, 1790–1930* (New York: Oxford University Press, 2001); Richard W. Judd, *Common Lands, Common People: The Origins of Conservation in Northern New England* (Cambridge: Harvard University Press, 1997); Richard White, *Land Use, Environment, and Social Change: The Shaping of Island County, Washington* (Seattle: University of Washington Press, 1980). Various perspectives on forest conservation are offered in Char Miller,

ed., *American Forests: Nature, Culture, and Politics* (Lawrence: University Press of Kansas, 1997).

2. I do not mean to discount the serious, sustained efforts made by many scholars, inside and outside the academy, to engage with conservation ideas. My criticism here is aimed chiefly at conservation as a public cause and at the leaders of it. As for the academic writing, it is prone to looking inward over time, both because academic evaluation standards are inward looking and because conservation leaders pay so little attention to it. A recent, apparently little-noted effort by academics to present ideas to conservation professionals is Ben A. Minteer and Robert E. Manning, eds., *Reconstructing Conservation: Finding Common Ground* (Washington, D.C.: Island Press, 2003).

3. References to leading historical works are included in the third entry in "Conservation's Central Readings: A Bibliographic Essay" (which highlights as exemplar Donald Worster, *The Wealth of Nature: Environmental History and the Ecological Imagination* [New York: Oxford University Press, 1993]).

4. The chief organizations and their work are considered in Richard Brewer, *Conservancy: The Land Trust Movement in America* (Hanover: Dartmouth University Press, 2003).

5. The emphasis of the Progressive Movement on controlling rampant individualism is considered in Michael McGerr, *A Fierce Discontent: The Rise and Fall of the Progressive Movement in America, 1870–1920* (New York: Free Press, 2003). Works on conservation during the period are cited in note 1 above.

Chapter 1
The Four Faces of Resistance

1. Wendell Berry, "Conserving Communities," in *Another Turn of the Crank* (Washington, D.C.: Counterpoint Press, 1995), 17.

2. Ibid. Berry's other commentaries on the global economy include "A Bad Big Idea" in *Sex, Economy, Freedom, and Community*

(New York: Pantheon Books, 1993), 45–51; "Farming and the Global Economy," in *Another Turn of the Crank*, 1–7; and "The Whole Horse," in Eric T. Freyfogle, ed., *The New Agrarianism: Land, Culture, and the Community of Life* (Washington, D.C.: Island Press, 2001), 63–79.

3. Donald Worster, *The Wealth of Nature: Environmental History and the Ecological Imagination* (New York: Oxford University Press, 1993); Donald Worster, *Dust Bowl: The Southern Plains in the 1930s* (New York: Oxford University Press, 1979).

4. Aldo Leopold, *A Sand County Almanac and Sketches Here and There* (New York: Oxford University Press, 1949), vii.

5. Ibid., 224–25.

6. Leopold's mature conservation thought, including his cultural criticism, is ably assessed in Julianne Lutz Newton, "The Commonweal of Life: Aldo Leopold and Land Health" (Ph.D. diss., University of Illinois at Urbana-Champaign, 2004; forthcoming from Island Press in 2006).

7. Leopold's emerging ecological orientation is described in Susan L. Flader, *Thinking Like a Mountain: Aldo Leopold and the Evolution of and Ecological Attitude toward Deer, Wolves, and Forests* (Columbia: University of Missouri Press, 1974).

8. A key essay recording Leopold's progress in providing an ecological grounding for his holistic thinking is "A Biotic View of Land" (1939), reprinted in Susan L. Flader and J. Baird Callicott, eds., *"The River of the Mother of God" and Other Essays by Aldo Leopold* (Madison: University of Wisconsin Press, 1991), 266–73. The scientific background of the essay is explored in detail in Newton, "The Commonweal of Life," 203–68.

9. Leopold, *A Sand County Almanac*, viii.

10. Aldo Leopold, "The Conservation League" and "Ecology, Philosophy, and Conservation," unpublished, undated manuscripts, Aldo Leopold Papers, series 10-6, box 16, University of Wisconsin Archives, Madison.

11. Aldo Leopold, "Threatened Species," in *The River of the Mother of God,* 230–31 (originally published 1936).

12. Aldo Leopold, "The Conservation Ethic," in *The River of the Mother of God,* 181, 187.

13. Aldo Leopold, "Land Pathology," in *The River of the Mother of God,* 212–13 (originally published 1935).

14. Ibid.

15. One of Leopold's clearest calls for conservationists to rally around the goal, and for ecologists to use their best guesses about what it meant for land to possess health, was published only half a century after his death. "The Land-Health Concept and Conservation," in J. Baird Callicott and Eric T. Freyfogle, eds., *For the Health of the Land: Previously Unpublished Essays and Other Writings,* by Aldo Leopold (Washington, D.C.: Island Press, 1999), 218–26 (originally written 1946). Leopold's writings on land health are carefully surveyed and assessed in Newton, "The Commonweal of Life," 411–53. Valuable perspectives on Leopold's thought are also presented in part 6 of J. Baird Callicott, *Beyond the Land Ethic: More Essays in Environmental Philosophy* (Albany: State University of New York Press, 1999).

16. Aldo Leopold, "Conservation: In Whole or in Part," in *The River of the Mother of God,* 311, 318 (originally written 1944).

17. "Land-Use and Democracy," in *The River of the Mother of God,* 295, 300 (originally published 1942).

18. "Biotic Land-Use," in *For the Health of the Land,* 198, 201.

19. Ibid., 205.

20. "Conservation," unpublished manuscript, attached to manuscript letter, Horace S. Fries to Aldo Leopold, August 8, 1946, Leopold Papers, series 10-1, box 1.

21. Leopold's use of the term *stability* and writings in which he used it in his shorthand description of healthy land (with particular reference to its ability to cycle nutrients efficiently) are considered in Newton, "The Commonweal of Life," 445–48, 457.

22. Ibid., 446–50. As Newton explains, Leopold used the term *integrity* in two related, overlapping ways. It primarily meant the biotic parts needed for land to retain its ability to cycle nutrients efficiently. Secondarily and as a prudential matter, it included the full range of species present in a location before industrial humans came along. Leopold at times used this latter definition because no one really knew what species were needed to keep land "stable"; it was thus wise to keep as many of the parts as possible, even though some of them perhaps were not needed. Ibid., 449.

23. *A Sand County Almanac,* 224–25.

24. Ibid., 221.

25. Leopold explored the economics of private lands conservation, beginning with his important essays "The Conservation Ethic" (1933), "Conservation Economics" (1934), and "Land Pathology" (1935), all now reprinted in *The River of the Mother of God.* His many unpublished manuscripts touching on the subject include (from Leopold Papers, series 10-6, boxes 16–18) "Armaments for Conservation," "Conservation and Politics," "Motives for Conservation," "Economics of the Wild," "Ecology and Economics in Land Use," and "Economics, Philosophy, and Land."

26. "Land Pathology," 215.

27. Ibid., 214.

28. "Conservation and Politics," unpublished, undated manuscript, Leopold Papers, series 10-6, box 16.

29. Aldo Leopold, "Pioneers and Gullies," in *The River of the Mother of God,* 106, 111 (originally published 1924).

30. *A Sand County Almanac,* 225.

31. Ibid., 210.

32. Aldo Leopold, "The State of the Profession," in *The River of the Mother of God,* 276, 280 (originally published 1940).

33. The leading secondary works on Berry are Andrew J. Angyal, *Wendell Berry* (New York: Twayne, 1995) and Kimberly K.

Smith, *Wendell Berry and the Agrarian Tradition: A Common Grace* (Lawrence: University Press of Kansas, 2003). Berry's various literary persona or voices are thoughtfully considered in Janet Goodrich, *The Unforeseen Self in the Works of Wendell Berry* (Columbia: University of Missouri Press, 2001). Various comments on Berry's writing and influence are collected in Paul Merchant, ed., *Wendell Berry* (Lewiston, Idaho: Confluence Press, 1991). Berry's most sustained meditation on the need to return to the Christian adage of loving one's neighbor, despite the ongoing decline of rural lands and rural communities, appears in fictional form in his novel *Jayber Crow* (Washington, D.C.: Counterpoint Press, 2000).

34. A biography of Berry has not yet appeared. Information about his life is included in many of his nonfiction writings as well as in Angyal, *Wendell Berry.*

35. Among the writings by Berry that draw on this experience is his essay "The Whole Horse."

36. Wendell Berry, "The Wild," in *Collected Poems, 1957–1982* (San Francisco: North Point Press, 1985), 19–20.

37. Wendell Berry, *The Long-Legged House* (New York: Harcourt, Brace and World, 1969), 118.

38. Wendell Berry, *Recollected Essays* (San Francisco: North Point Press, 1981), ix.

39. Wendell Berry, *A Continuous Harmony: Essays Cultural and Agricultural* (New York: Harcourt Brace Jovanovich, 1972), 164; Berry, *Sex, Economy, Freedom, and Community,* 14–15, 40; Wendell Berry, *What Are People For?* (San Francisco: North Point Press, 1990), 149, 206–7.

40. Albert Howard, *The Soil and Health: A Study of Organic Agriculture* (New York: Devin-Adair, 1947), 11. Berry's uses of the quotation include *What Are People For?* 149; *Another Turn of the Crank,* 89–90.

41. Wendell Berry, "Health Is Membership," in *Another Turn of the Crank,* 86, 90.

42. Among the writings in which Berry explores the themes is "Conservation and Local Economy," in *Sex, Economy, Freedom, and Community,* 3–18.

43. Ibid.; Berry, "Conserving Communities," 8.

44. He develops the issue in many writings, including "Conserving Forest Communities," in *Another Turn of the Crank,* 25–45.

45. Wendell Berry, "Private Property and the Common Wealth," in *Another Turn of the Crank,* 46, 48.

46. For instance, "Conservation Is Good Work," in *Sex, Economy, Freedom, and Community,* 27, 39–40 ("And, of course, in talking about the formation of local economies capable of using an earthly place without ruining it, we are talking about the reformation of people").

47. For instance, "Private Property and the Common Wealth," 47 ("My hope, I must say, subsists on an extremely meager diet—a reducer's diet"); "The Whole Horse," 75.

48. Leopold died in mid-stride in terms of his professional work, with many ongoing projects designed to expand his understandings and clarify his conservation thought. Newton, "The Commonweal of Life," 254–67, 461–67.

49. Aldo Leopold, "The Ecological Conscience," in *The River of the Mother of God,* 340–46.

50. A typical treatment is Barry C. Field, *Environmental Economics: An Introduction,* 2nd ed. (Boston: Irwin McGraw-Hill, 1997), 69–77.

51. On the challenges to sound land use posed by fragmentation, see Eric T. Freyfogle, *The Land We Share: Private Property and the Common Good* (Washington, D.C.: Island Press, 2003), 157–78.

52. A good consideration is Herman E. Daly and Joshua Farley, *Ecological Economics: Principles and Applications* (Washington, D.C.: Island Press, 2004), 157–219.

53. An important work addressing common-property management possibilities is Elinor Ostrom, *Governing the Commons:*

The Evolution of Institutions for Collective Action (Cambridge: Cambridge University Press, 1990).

54. Two of the most careful studies are Deborah Lynn Guber, *The Grassroots of a Green Revolution: Polling America on the Environment* (Cambridge: MIT Press, 2003) and Willett Kempton, James S. Boster, and Jennifer A. Hartley, *Environmental Values in American Culture* (Cambridge: MIT Press, 1995).

55. A useful survey of shifting American thoughts about liberty is Michael G. Kammen, *Spheres of Liberty: Changing Perceptions of Liberty in American Culture* (Madison: University of Wisconsin Press, 1986).

56. A useful introduction is Anthony Arblaster, *Democracy*, 2nd ed. (Minneapolis: University of Minnesota Press, 1994). America's shifting ideas on the subject are considered in Robert H. Wiebe, *Self-Rule: A Cultural History of American Democracy* (Chicago: University of Chicago Press, 1996).

57. Useful surveys of ideas on property in the United States include Gregory Alexander, *Commodity and Propriety: Competing Visions of Property in American Legal Theory, 1776–1970* (Chicago: University of Chicago Press, 1997); William B. Scott, *In Pursuit of Happiness: American Conceptions of Property from the Seventeenth to the Twentieth Century* (Bloomington: Indiana University Press, 1977).

58. An example is Thomas W. Merrill, "Private Property and the Politics of Environmental Protection," *Harvard Journal of Law and Public Policy* 28 (2004): 69–80 (contending that in terms of the causes of varying environmental conditions, the "only difference" between eastern and western Europe was the existence of private property in the West). Merrill neither notes the existence of private property in the East nor questions how closely the private property of western Europe resembles private property in the United States.

59. John Echeverria, "The Politics of Property Rights," *Oklahoma Law Review* 50 (1997): 351–75.

60. Differing visions of private landownership are considered in Eric T. Freyfogle, *Bounded People, Boundless Lands: Envisioning a New Land Ethic* (Washington, D.C.: Island Press, 1998), 91–113.

61. The ambiguities within the idea of equality are considered in Peter Westen, *Speaking of Equality* (Princeton: Princeton University Press, 1990).

62. A similar criticism of environmentalism, highlighting its failure to respond to cultural challenges, is Samuel Hays, *A History of Environmental Politics since 1945* (Pittsburgh: University of Pittsburgh Press, 2000), 223–24.

63. Aldo Leopold, "The Conservation Ethic," 187.

64. There are important exceptions, some of which are noted in entry 12 of "Conservation's Central Readings."

65. As Richard Lazarus notes, the aggregate benefits of federal environmental programs appear to significantly exceed their costs. The difficulty arises (as Aldo Leopold had noted) because the benefits do not go to those who incur the costs (or, as it might more aptly be stated, because those who must halt their patterns of harming other people are not reimbursed by their victims for the costs of doing so). Richard J. Lazarus, *The Making of Environmental Law* (Chicago: University of Chicago Press, 2004), 24–28.

66. An introduction is offered in John Gray, *Liberalism* (Minneapolis: University of Minnesota Press, 1986).

67. A perceptive exploration that reconciles environmentalism with liberalism—although only after refining the latter idea—is Mark Sagoff, *The Economy of the Earth: Philosophy, Law, and the Environment* (Cambridge: Cambridge University Press, 1988), 146–70.

68. Liberalism, of course, is diversely defined. Environmentalism does fit within recent definitions that focus on the use of government to promote social progress and contain the market. As for the classical definition, opponents of environmentalism

are more likely to rate higher as liberals, a point thoughtfully developed in C. A. Bowers, *Mindful Conservatism: Rethinking the Ideological and Educational Basis of an Ecologically Sustainable Future* (Lanham, Md.: Rowman and Littlefield, 2003).

69. Aldo Leopold, "The Farm Wildlife Program: A Self-Scrutiny," unpublished, undated manuscript (circa 1937), Leopold Papers, series 10-6, box 16.

70. Freyfogle, *Bounded People, Boundless Lands,* 75–90.

71. Useful sources for this work include Lester Brown, *Eco-Economy: Building an Economy for the Earth* (New York: W. W. Norton, 2001); Brian Czech, *Shoveling Fuel for a Runaway Train: Errant Economists, Shameful Spenders, and a Plan to Stop Them All* (Berkeley: University of California Press, 2000); Herman E. Daly and John B. Cobb, *For the Common Good: Redirecting the Economy toward Community, the Environment, and a Sustainable Future,* 2nd ed. (Boston: Beacon Press, 1994); Eric A. Davidson, *You Can't Eat GNP: Economics as if Ecology Mattered* (Cambridge, Mass.: Perseus, 2000).

72. A standard libertarian perspective on ownership, portraying property rights in a way strongly slanted toward development and industrial land uses, is Richard A. Epstein, *Takings: Private Property and the Power of Eminent Domain* (Cambridge: Harvard University Press, 1985).

Chapter 2
Five Paths and Their Values

1. An earlier attempt to categorize varieties of environmental law scholarship is J. B. Ruhl, "The Case of the Speluncean Polluters: Six Themes of Environmental Law, Policy, and Ethics," *Environmental Law* 27 (1997), 343–73. Ruhl's categories are similar except that he does not include among his approaches an ecological orientation similar to the one I have termed advocates for the land community.

2. Although the emergence of environmental law has received scholarly attention, the scholarly aspect of it has not become an important subject of independent study. For many years the leading historian of environmental law and policy has been Samuel P. Hays, whose work has been sadly overlooked by legal scholars. His major works are *Beauty, Health, and Permanence: Environmental Politics in the United States, 1955–1985* (Cambridge: Cambridge University Press, 1987); *Explorations in Environmental History* (Pittsburgh: University of Pittsburgh Press, 1998); and *A History of Environmental Politics since 1945* (Pittsburgh: University of Pittsburgh Press, 2000). A lawyer's view of the subject—covering legal developments in useful detail but paying little attention to the environmental movement and cultural politics—is offered in Richard J. Lazarus, *The Making of Environmental Law* (Chicago: University of Chicago Press, 2004). Journalistic histories of the environmental movement have become numerous, though none quite compares with the work of Hays. Prominent works include Philip Shabecoff, *A Fierce Green Fire: The American Environmental Movement* (New York: Hill and Wang, 1993); Robert Gottleib, *Forcing the Spring: The Transformation of the American Environmental Movement* (Washington, D.C.: Island Press, 1993). A narrow, sensitive study is Adam Rome, *The Bulldozer in the Countryside: Suburban Sprawl and the Rise of American Environmentalism* (Cambridge: Cambridge University Press, 2001).

3. Because the aim here is to isolate scholarly approaches or types, not to probe the scholarly work of any particular scholars, a difficulty arises in citing scholars as examples of the approaches. Scholars inevitably have their eccentricities and display different attitudes in different works. With these caveats in mind, it might be said that the following scholars typically illustrate the five types: libertarians (Richard Epstein and a suite of newer legal scholars, including Jonathan Adler

and Gary Marchant), simple fixers (law and economics scholars, from Terry Anderson to Richard Revesz), dispute
resolvers (Richard Stewart and Cass Sunstein, among many
others), progressive reformers (Dan Farber, Dan Tarlock,
Nick Robinson, and many others), and land community
advocates (Oliver Houck and Joseph Sax).

4. These ideas, of course, are largely borrowed by legal scholars
from writings in economics. Leading economic texts from an
ecological perspective—which often cast doubt on even the
theoretical possibility of correcting market failures—are mentioned in the final entry of recommended readings "Conservation's Central Readings: A Bibliographic Essay."

5. As should be clear, I do not mean to suggest that legal scholars
routinely (or ever) discuss these moral and intellectual issues.
My claim instead is that they base their work on embedded
presumptions about them, and that these presumptions can
and should be teased apart for separate consideration.

6. Citizen involvement is by no means an easy undertaking, of
course, subject to takeover by economic interests that have the
most at stake. Some of the dangers are considered in Holly
Doremus, "Preserving Citizen Participation in the Era of
Reinvention: The Endangered Species Act Example," *Ecology
Law Quarterly* 25 (1999): 707–17; Bradley C. Karkkainen,
"Collaborative Ecosystem Governance: Scale, Compexity,
and Dynamism," *Virginia Environmental Law Journal* 21
(2002): 189–243; Rena I. Steinzor, "The Corruption of Civic
Environmentalism," *Environmental Law Reporter* 30 (2002):
10909–21.

7. Much libertarian writing studiously avoids the term *community*,
presumably because of its favorable connotations. Richard A.
Epstein, *Takings: Private Property and the Power of Eminent
Domain* (Cambridge: Harvard University Press, 1985) is illus-
trative linguistically in how it carefully describes problems as
clashes between the individual and the "state"—the latter term

vaguely resonant of fascism and carrying stronger negative connotations than "government."

8. A much fuller explanation (and criticism) of this worldview is
set forth in David Ehrenfeld, *The Arrogance of Humanism*
(Oxford: Oxford University Press, 1981). The confusion
about the underlying values, greatly exacerbated by confused
rhetoric and the misuse of political labels, is considered in
C. A. Bowers, *Mindful Conservatism: Rethinking the Ideological and Educational Basis of an Ecologically Sustainable Future*
(Lanham, Md.: Rowman and Littlefield, 2003).

9. These ideas, of course, appear most vividly in the writings of
Aldo Leopold, which continue to surface in legal scholarly
writing. Amy J. Wildermuth, "Eco-Pragmatism and Ecology:
What's Leopold Got to Do with It?" *Minnesota Law Review*
87 (2003): 1145–71.

10. The idea is promoted in Carolyn Raffensperger and Joel
Tickner, eds., *Protecting Public Health and the Environment:
Implementing the Precautionary Principle* (Washington, D.C.:
Island Press, 1999).

11. This reasoning appears prominently in the work of Wendell
Berry and Wes Jackson, among many others. Eric T. Freyfogle,
*Bounded People, Boundless Lands: Envisioning a New Land
Ethic* (Washington, D.C.: Island Press, 1998), 131–36.

12. This line of thought permeates serious conservation writing outside the law—far more than within legal writing. The recommended readings described in "Conservation's Central Readings"
are, by and large, variations and expansions on this point.

13. An exception is Rutherford H. Platt, "The Geographical Basis
of Land Use Law," in Gary L. Thompson, Fred M. Shelley
and Chand Wije, eds., *Geography, Environment, and American
Law* (Boulder: University of Colorado Press, 1997).

14. By "environmental movement" I mean here not just (or even
principally) the work of public-interest conservation groups,
important as they have been, but the larger shift in values and

sensibilities that helped give such groups strength and that generated public support for limits on market operations. A survey is offered in Shabecoff, *A Fierce Green Fire.*

15. Richard J. Lazarus, "Environmental Scholarship and the Harvard Difference," *Harvard Environmental Law Review* 21 (1999): 354–55.

Chapter 3
The Lure of the Garden

1. I offer comments on the first two of these approaches in *The Land We Share: Private Property and the Common Good* (Washington, D.C.: Island Press, 2003), 157–201.

2. The opposition is surveyed in Samuel P. Hays, *A History of Environmental Politics since 1945* (Pittsburgh: University of Pittsburgh Press, 2000), 109–21.

3. René Dubos, *The Wooing of Earth: New Perspectives of Man's Use of Nature* (London: Athlone Press, 1980).

4. Michael Pollan, *Second Nature: A Gardener's Education* (New York: Dell, 1992). Subsequent references to this work will be given in the text.

5. Aldo Leopold, "The Farmer as a Conservationist," in Susan L. Flader and J. Baird Callicott, *"The River of the Mother of God" and Other Essays by Aldo Leopold* (Madison: University of Wisconsin Press, 1991), 255–65. Subsequent references to this work will be given in the text.

6. The importance of the essay in Leopold's thought is considered in Julianne Lutz Newton, "The Commonweal of Life: Aldo Leopold and Land Health" (Ph.D. diss., University of Illinois at Urbana-Champaign, 2004; forthcoming from Island Press in 2006), 399–405.

7. Left unnoted, of course, is the evident practicality of the arrangement as well as the possibility that the environmentalist-gardener has his own aesthetic standards.

8. Pollan cites law professor Christopher Stone's argument in favor of legal standing for "trees" (by which Stone meant forests as communities, not individual plants) in a way that apparently recognizes the vast difference between legal standing and moral rights (203–4). So strong is Pollan's anthropocentrism that even a single human—any human, it appears—clearly outweighs morally even "the last few grizzlies." "We could end up wrecking liberalism," he asserts, were we to recognize moral value in any nonhuman life (204).

9. Samuel P. Hays, *Beauty, Health, and Permanence: Environmental Politics in the United States, 1955–1985* (Cambridge: Cambridge University Press, 1987).

10. The early part of the story is told in Paul S. Sutter, *Driven Wild: How the Fight against Automobiles Launched the Modern Wilderness Movement* (Seattle: University of Washington Press, 2002).

11. Two of the most careful studies of public views are Deborah Lynn Guber, *The Grassroots of a Green Revolution: Polling America on the Environment* (Cambridge: MIT Press, 2003), and Willett Kempton, James S. Boster, and Jennifer A. Hartley, *Environmental Values in American Culture* (Cambridge: MIT Press, 1995).

12. Pollan uses the example of gravity (objects falling down) to argue that "nature *loves* straight lines" (289).

13. Similarly, we have Pollan's contention that "Thoreau, in fact, was the last important American writer on nature to have anything to say about gardening" (4).

14. For instance, "Power Steer," *New York Times Magazine,* March 31, 2002, section 6, p. 44.

Chapter 4
Back to Sustainability

1. Many of the ideas and observations in this chapter are drawn from Julianne Lutz Newton and Eric T. Freyfogle,

"Sustainability: A Dissent," *Conservation Biology* 19 (2005): 23–32. I thank my coauthor for allowing me to draw freely on this piece and for many useful discussions on the topic.

2. For instance, John Cairns, Jr., "The Zen of Sustainable Use of the Planet: Steps on the Path to Enlightenment," *Population and Environment: A Journal of Interdisciplinary Studies* 20 (1998): 109–23; J. Baird Callicott and Karen Mumford, "Ecological Sustainability as a Conservation Concept," *Conservation Biology* 11 (1997): 32–40 (criticizing the term as "hopelessly tainted"); Robert T. Lackey, "Seven Pillars of Ecosystem Management," *Landscape and Urban Planning* 40 (1998): 21–30; Bryan G. Norton, "Sustainability, Human Welfare, and Ecosystem Health," in *Searching for Sustainability: Interdisciplinary Essays in the Philosophy of Conservation Biology* (Cambridge: Cambridge University Press, 2003), 168–82 ("Nobody opposes it because nobody knows exactly what it entails"); Thomas M. Parris, "Toward a Sustainability Transition," *Environment* 45 (2003): 12–22. The term *sustainable development* has been subjected to even harsher criticism. Bill Willers, "Sustainable Development: A New World Deception," *Conservation Biology* 8 (1994): 1148 ("[S]ustainable development is one of the most insidious and manipulable ideas to appear in decades"); Donald Worster, "The Shaky Ground of Sustainable Development," in *The Wealth of Nature: Environmental History and the Ecological Imagination* (New York: Oxford University Press, 1993), 153 ("irredeemable for environmentalist use" and subject to "deep flaws").

3. For instance, Christine Padoch and Robin R. Sears, "Conserving Concepts: In Praise of Sustainability," *Conservation Biology* 19 (2005): 39–41.

4. David Ehrenfeld, "Sustainability: Living with the Imperfections," *Conservation Biology* 19 (2005): 34–35 ("If the idea of sustainability is invoked, independently, by those whose

interests are solely in human survival, by those whose landscape of concern features humans embedded in the biosphere, and by those whose cares are entirely for nonhuman nature, so much the better. Perhaps their shared fondness for the word sustainability will provide enough common ground so that they can begin to talk to one another").

5. Worster, "The Shaky Ground of Sustainable Development," 143–45.

6. Samuel P. Hays, *Conservation and the Gospel of Efficiency: The Progressive Conservation Movement, 1890–1920* (New York: Atheneum, 1969).

7. Wes Jackson, "Toward a Sustainable Agriculture," *Not Man Apart* (November–December 1978): 4–6.

8. Steven Stoll, *Larding the Lean Earth: Soil and Society in Nineteenth-Century America* (New York: Hill and Wang, 2002).

9. Wendell Berry, *The Unsettling of America: Culture and Agriculture* (San Francisco: Sierra Club Books, 1977).

10. Worster, "The Shaky Ground of Sustainable Development," 143.

11. World Commission on Environment and Development, *Our Common Future* (Oxford: Oxford University Press, 1987), 43.

12. For instance, Report of the National Commission on the Environment, *Choosing a Sustainable Future* (Washington, D.C.: Island Press, 1993); Juliet Schor and Betsy Taylor, *Sustainable Planet: Solutions for the Twenty-first Century* (Boston: Beacon Press, 2002).

13. Wes Jackson, *New Roots for Agriculture,* rev. ed. (Lincoln: University of Nebraska Press, 1985), 11–60. A more recent critical assessment of contemporary agriculture is David Tilman et al., "Agricultural Sustainability and Intensive Production Practices," *Nature* 418 (2002): 671–77.

14. Gregory McIsaac, "Sustainability and Sustainable Agriculture," in Gregory McIsaac and William R. Edwards, eds., *Sustainable Agriculture in the American Midwest: Lessons from the*

Past, Prospects for the Future (Urbana: University of Illinois Press, 1994), 27–28.

15. Richard P. Gale and Sheila M. Cordray, "Making Sense of Sustainability: Nine Answers to 'What Should Be Sustained?'" *Rural Sociology* 59 (1994): 311–32.

16. World Commission on Environment and Development, *Our Common Future,* 43.

17. Ibid.

18. The Brundtland Report does declare that "at a minimum, sustainable development must not endanger the natural systems that support life on Earth: the atmosphere, the waters, the soils, and the living beings." Ibid., 45. The goal sounds worthy enough, but we are left to wonder how this idea fits together with the term's core definition, particularly its stress on meeting the needs of the world's poor, and whether it implies a duty among the rich to share with the poor. In its context the sentence appears gratuitous; it is not part of the definition of sustainable development but instead merely a side aspiration, a hope that, someday, somehow, our methods of promoting sustainable development will respect the natural fabric.

19. The philosophical literature on future generations is vast. A good entry point, geared to the idea of sustainability, is Bryan G. Norton, "Intergenerational Equity and Sustainability," in *Searching for Sustainability: Interdisciplinary Essays in the Philosophy of Conservation Biology* (Cambridge: Cambridge University Press, 2003), 420–55. Norton—himself a leading advocate of an environmental ethic focused on future generations—offers a similar observation on the inattention given to this core element of sustainability: "While it seems clear that calls for sustainable activities and policies must rest on an obligation of current people to future generations, philosophers have contributed little to the ongoing policy debates regarding how to define and measure these key

terms." A good collection of perspectives on the issue is Ernest Partridge, ed., *Responsibilities to Future Generations: Environmental Ethics* (Buffalo: Prometheus Books, 1981).

20. Wynn Calder and Richard M. Clugston, "Progress toward Sustainability in Higher Education," *Environmental Law Reporter* 33 (2003): 10003–22. The President's Council on Sustainable Development concluded its work in May 1999 with its report *Towards a Sustainable America: Advancing Prosperity, Opportunity, and a Healthy Environment for the 21st Century* (1999).

21. This is the core idea of the Brundtland Report, World Commission on Environment and Development, *Our Common Future,* 43–46. An obvious problem arises with respect to nonrenewable resources, which can be used only by consuming them. On this issue, the Brundtland Report proposes (as do other studies) that rates of consumption be tied to the pace of efforts to find substitutes. "In general the rate of depletion should take into account the criticality of that resource, the availability of technologies for minimizing depletion, and the likelihood of substitutes being available. . . . With minerals and fossil fuels, the rate of depletion and the emphasis on recycling and economy of use should be calibrated to ensure that the resource does not run out before acceptable substitutes are available." Ibid., 46.

22. Worster, "The Shaky Ground of Sustainable Development," 144. Worster's essay develops a thesis similar to the one presented here: "Like most popular slogans, sustainable development wears thin after a while, revealing a lack of any new core idea. Although it seems to have gained a wide acceptance, it has done so by sacrificing real substance. Worse yet, the slogan may turn out to be irredeemable for environmentalist use because it may inescapably lead us back to using a narrow economic language, to relying on production as the standard of judgment, and to following the progressive

materialist world-view in approaching and utilizing the earth, all of which was precisely what environmentalism once sought to overthrow."

23. Among the interests resisting planned, multiple-use waterway management was the Army Corps of Engineers, which opposed the shift in part to protect its organizational independence and in part because it feared for the primacy of navigation among waterway uses. Hays, *Conservation and the Gospel of Efficiency,* 199–218.

24. Ibid., 1–4; Gifford Pinchot, *The Fight for Conservation* (New York: Doubleday, Page, 1910).

25. The story of wildlife conservation is recounted in John F. Reiger, *American Sportsmen and the Origins of Conservation,* 3rd ed. (Corvallis: Oregon State University, 2000); James B. Trefethen, *An American Crusade for Wildlife* (New York: Winchester Press, 1975); Gregory J. Dehler, "An American Crusader: William Temple Hornaday and Wildlife Protection in America, 1840–1940" (Ph.D. diss., Lehigh University, 2001).

26. P. A. Larkin, "An Epitaph for the Concept of Maximum Sustained Yield," *Transactions of the American Fisheries Society* 106 (1977): 1, 3.

27. At the forefront of this recognition was Aldo Leopold, whose intellectual progress on the issue is ably recounted in Susan L. Flader, *Thinking Like a Mountain: Aldo Leopold and the Evolution of an Ecological Attitude toward Deer, Wolves, and Forests* (Columbia: University of Missouri Press, 1974), 122–67.

28. John von Neumann and Oskar Morgenstern, *Theory of Games and Economic Behavior* (Princeton: Princeton University Press, 1953).

29. David Ehrenfeld, *The Arrogance of Humanism* (Oxford: Oxford University Press, 1981), 112.

30. Hays, *Conservation and the Gospel of Efficiency,* 91–121.

31. Julianne Lutz Newton, "The Commonweal of Life: Aldo Leopold and Land Health" (Ph.D. diss., University of Illinois at Urbana-Champaign, 2004; forthcoming from Island Press in 2006), 183–99, 406–53.

32. Thomas Dunlap, *Saving America's Wildlife: Ecology and the American Mind, 1850–1990* (Princeton: Princeton University Press, 1991).

33. Robert Croker, *Pioneer Ecologist: The Life and Work of Victor Ernest Shelford, 1877–1968* (Washington, D.C.: Smithsonian Institute Press, 1991), 120–44.

34. Paul. S. Sutter, *Driven Wild: How the Fight against Automobiles Launched the Modern Wilderness Movement* (Seattle: University of Washington Press, 2002).

35. Larry Anderson, *Benton MacKaye: Conservationist, Planner, and Creator of the Appalachian Trail* (Baltimore: Johns Hopkins University Press, 2002), 371–79.

36. Benton MacKaye, *The New Exploration: A Philosophy of Regional Planning* (Urbana: University of Illinois Press, 1962), 160.

37. Newton, "The Commonweal of Life," 120–65, 203–68.

38. Donald Worster, *Dust Bowl: The Southern Plains in the 1930s* (Oxford: Oxford University Press, 1979), 182–209.

39. Stoll, *Larding the Lean Earth,* 31–41, 134–40.

40. Worster, *Dust Bowl,* 210–26.

41. Ibid., 188–96.

42. Mark Luccarelli, *Lewis Mumford and the Ecological Region: The Politics of Planning* (New York: Guilford Press, 1995), 56–83.

43. William Vogt, *Road to Survival* (New York: William Sloane, 1948).

44. Dunlap, *Saving America's Wildlife.*

45. A thoughtful summary of differing perspectives is contained in J. Baird Callicott, Larry B. Crowder, and Karen Mumford,

"Current Normative Concepts in Conservation," *Conservation Biology* 13 (1999): 22–35.

46. The struggles to do so, and the ways in which scientific thought was intermingled with social and political thought, are explored in Donald Worster, *Nature's Economy: A History of Ecological Ideas,* 2nd ed. (Cambridge: Cambridge University Press, 1994), 340–443.

47. Gretchen C. Daily and Katherine Ellison, *The New Economy of Nature* (Washington, D.C.: Island Press, 2002); Paul Hawken, Amory Lovins, and L. Hunter Lovins, *Natural Capitalism: Creating the Next Industrial Revolution* (Boston: Back Bay Books, 2000).

48. Nicky Chambers, Craig Simmons, and Mathis Wackernagel, *Sharing Nature's Interest: Ecological Footprints as an Indicator of Sustainability* (London: Earthscan, 2000); Mathis Wackernagel and William E. Rees, *Our Ecological Footprint: Reducing Human Impact on the Earth* (Philadelphia: New Society, 1996).

49. A useful overview of the vast literature is Peter S. Wenz, *Environmental Ethics Today* (New York: Oxford University Press, 2001).

50. A similar conclusion is reached in Worster, "The Shaky Ground of Sustainable Development," 153–55.

51. A typical broad use of the term is Schor and Taylor, *Sustainable Planet.* The term *sustainable development,* of course, began its life with this kind of breadth. World Commission on Environment and Development, *Our Common Future,* 43.

52. Hays, *Conservation and the Gospel of Efficiency,* 9–15.

53. Worster, *Dust Bowl,* 187–96; Lewis C. Gray, "The Problem of Agricultural Settlement and Resettlement in the United States," *Southwestern Political Science Quarterly* 2 (1921): 125–51.

54. Sutter, *Driven Wild,* 54–99.

55. A study prepared by the Office of Management and Budget, "Draft Report to Congress on the Costs and Benefits of Federal Regulations," 67 *Fed. Reg.* 15014, 15037 (March 28, 2002), table 11, estimated that as of September 2001, the total aggregated annual costs associated with all major federal environmental regulations had a range with a midpoint of $163 billion; the range for the total annual benefits had a midpoint of $950 billion.

56. David Mobert, "The Wal-Mart Effect," *In These Times,* July 5, 2004.

57. Jeremy Rifkin, *Beyond Beef: The Rise and Fall of the Cattle Culture* (New York: E. P. Dutton, 1992). The larger contexts of industrial agriculture are considered in Terence J. Centner, *Empty Pastures: Confined Animals and the Transformation of the Rural Landscape* (Urbana: University of Illinois Press, 2004).

Chapter 5
What Is Good Land Use?

1. A fourth approach, used by many social scientists and geographers, is to turn the issue of good land use into a question of process, allowing the people who live in a place to decide for themselves what is good. By definition, whatever the outcome of the proper process is then defined as good land use. The process could entail simply canvassing people individually to find out what they want; it could entail instead some mechanism by which people get together to act collectively. In neither case does the researcher pass judgment (or even have a basis for passing judgment) on the land-use preferences that emerge from the process.

2. Many of the ideas in this chapter first appeared in different form in Eric T. Freyfogle and Julianne Lutz Newton, "Putting Science in Its Place," *Conservation Biology* 16 (2002): 863–73, and I thank my coauthor for allowing me to draw freely on it.

3. On the direct links between nature and human health, see Michael McCally, ed., *Life Support: The Environment and Human Health* (Cambridge: MIT Press, 2002); Dade W. Moeller, *Environmental Health,* 3rd ed. (Cambridge: Harvard University Press, 2004).

4. The market's various shortcomings are considered in Herman E. Daly and Joshua Farley, *Ecological Economics: Principles and Applications* (Washington, D.C.: Island Press, 2004), 157–219.

5. The field is surveyed in Bryan G. Norton, *Toward Unity among Environmentalists* (Oxford: Oxford University Press, 1991); Peter S. Wenz, *Environmental Ethics Today* (Oxford: Oxford University Press, 2001).

6. A careful, detailed study—though now a bit dated—is Willett Kempton, James S. Boster, and Jennifer A. Hartley, *Environmental Values in American Culture* (Cambridge: MIT Press, 1996), 111, which shows 87 percent of the public agreeing that "all species have a right to evolve without human interference" (versus 82 percent support by Sierra Club members) and 90 percent of the public saying that "preventing species extinction should be our highest environmental priority" (versus 78 percent support by Sierra Club members).

7. This reasoning appears prominently in the writings of Wendell Berry, including his essay "Nature as Measure" in *What Are People For?* (San Francisco: North Point Press, 1990), 204–10.

8. Carolyn Raffensperger and Joel Tickner, eds., *Protecting Public Health and the Environment: Implementing the Precautionary Principle* (Washington, D.C.: Island Press, 1999).

9. William P. Rodgers, *Environmental Law,* 2nd ed. (St. Paul: West, 1994), 800–970.

10. Dale D. Goble and Eric T. Freyfogle, *Wildlife Law: Cases and Materials* (New York: Foundation Press, 2002), 1220–51.

11. James T. O'Reilly, *Food and Drug Administration,* 2nd ed. (New York: McGraw-Hill, 1995 and 2004 supplement), 11-32 to 11-39, 14-8 to 14-13.

12. At times the level of proof seems to be set so high that no evidence would satisfy it. See, for instance, Alex Avery and Dennis Avery, "Bring Back DDT, and Save Lives," *Wall Street Journal,* July 28, 2000 ("[W]e have yet to find a single significant health threat from DDT use even after 40 years of exhaustive research").

13. Rachel Carson, *Silent Spring* (New York: Houghton Mifflin, 1962).

14. Thomas Dunlap, *DDT: Scientists, Citizens, and Public Policy* (Princeton: Princeton University Press, 1983).

15. David Pimentel, Laura Westra, and Reed F. Noss, eds., *Ecological Integrity: Integrating Environment, Conservation, and Health* (Washington, D.C.: Island Press, 2000); Paul L. Angermeier and James R. Karr, "Biological Integrity versus Biological Diversity as Policy Directives," *BioScience* 44 (1994): 690–97; Paul L. Angermeier, "The Natural Imperative for Biological Conservation," *Conservation Biology* 14 (2000): 373–81; J. Baird Callicott, Larry B. Crowder, and Karen Mumford, "Current Normative Concepts in Conservation," *Conservation Biology* 13 (1999): 22–35.

16. Samuel P. Hays, *Conservation and the Gospel of Efficiency: The Progressive Conservation Movement, 1890–1920* (New York: Atheneum, 1969), 2–4.

17. Two essays by Baird Callicott explore the issue in the context of land ethics. J. Baird Callicott, "Hume's *Is/Ought* Dichotomy and the Relation of Ecology to Leopold's Land Ethic," in *In Defense of the Land Ethic: Essays in Environmental Philosophy* (Albany: State University of New York Press, 1989), 117–27; J. Baird Callicott, "Just the Facts, Ma'am," in *Beyond the Land Ethic: More Essays in Environmental Philosophy* (Albany: State University of New York Press, 1999), 79–97.

18. Foreman's ideas are set forth in Dave Foreman, *Rewilding North America: A Vision for Conservation in the 21st Century* (Washington, D.C.: Island Press, 2004).

19. There are important exceptions. A fine inquiry is undertaken in David Ehrenfeld, *The Arrogance of Humanism* (Oxford: Oxford University Press, 1981), 177–211. A useful summary of considerations appears in Reed F. Noss and Allen Y. Cooperrider, *Saving Nature's Legacy: Protecting and Restoring Biodiversity* (Washington, D.C.: Island Press, 1994), 17–23.

20. William R. Jordan III, *The Sunflower Forest: Ecological Restoration and the New Communion with Nature* (Berkeley: University of California Press, 2003). Various perspectives are gathered in A. Dwight Baldwin, Judith De Luce, and Carl Pletsch, eds., *Beyond Preservation: Restoring and Inventing Landscapes* (Minneapolis: University of Minnesota Press, 1994).

21. Jordan, *The Sunflower Forest,* 195–204.

22. William Jordan contends that restoration as he defines it can have distinct ecological content. It entails "bringing the whole system back to a former condition whatever that might happen to be—not just those features we find beautiful, interesting, or useful but also those that we consider uninteresting, useless, ugly, repulsive, or even dangerous." Ibid., 22. It is up to the restorationist, however, to select the "former condition" that will be the goal, and as Jordan notes, this may or may not be a natural condition that is ecologically healthy. Jordan cites as example the restoration of a Nazi concentration camp, a project that involved taking out trees and other plants "in order to return a field of cinders to its former, ecologically sterile condition." As the example illustrates, "restoration is not the same thing as making a landscape 'better' or 'improving' it." The key element of restoration for Jordan is the attempt "to compensate for novel or 'outside' influences" on a given place so as to return it to some chosen historical condition. If the chosen state is one without humans, then all human influences must be removed, though, as Jordan notes, given that "everything interacts with and influences every-

thing else, preservation of an ecosystem is ultimately impossible." Ibid., 23. Restoration as thus defined stands apart "from other restorative forms of land management such as rehabilitation (the restoration of function, or certain selected functions), or reclamation (rehabilitation, usually from a profoundly disturbed condition resulting from an activity such as mining or construction), or even healing (the restoration of health)." Ibid., 22–23.

23. I do not mean to say that particular restoration projects are always or even usually poorly explained in terms of their benefits to the functioning of human-occupied lands. The defect lies at the top level, in the language of restoration itself, which can share many of the defects of sustainability. Just as sustainability fails to tell us what is being sustained, restoration doesn't indicate what is being restored and why. Particularly as defined by Jordan, the idea and rhetoric of restoration do not give us answers, and it is up to the individual restorationist to choose. The answers are particularly unclear when a restorationist like Jordan feels free to select among any prior historical condition.

Chapter 6
Conservation's Core Tasks

1. Samuel P. Hays, *A History of Environmental Politics since 1945* (Pittsburgh: University of Pittsburgh Press, 2000), 227 ("The World of contemporary environmental affairs is badly in need of individuals who would reflect on the whole and institutions that could provide the resources for them to do so. . . . Few have time or interest enough to become well informed or to pursue careful understanding of what is one of the most important developments in society and politics in both America and the entire world").

2. Others have made the same observation: for instance, Richard Andrews, *Managing the Environment, Managing Ourselves* (New Haven: Yale University Press, 1999), 370 ("What is missing from American environmental policy is a coherent vision of common environmental good that is sufficiently compelling to generate sustained public support for government action to achieve it").

3. Robert Costanza, Bryan G. Norton, and Benjamin D. Haskell, *Ecosystem Health: New Goals for Environmental Management* (Washington, D.C.: Island Press, 1992).

4. Donald Worster, "The Ecology of Order and Chaos," in *The Wealth of Nature: Environmental History and the Ecological Imagination* (Oxford: Oxford University Press, 1993), 162–70 (noting the declining emphasis on ecosystem in leading ecology texts, including one that does not mention it). Shifts in thought about ecosystems are summarized in Robert P. McIntosh, *The Background of Ecology: Concept and Theory* (Cambridge: Cambridge University Press, 1985), 234–42.

5. J. Baird Callicott, "Aldo Leopold's Concept of Ecosystem Health," in *Beyond the Land Ethic: More Essays in Environmental Philosophy* (Albany: State University of New York Press, 1999), 333–45. Dictionaries commonly include among the definitions of the term "vigor or vitality."

6. Leopold's ideas about land health and the examples he drew on are considered in Julianne Lutz Newton, "The Commonweal of Life: Aldo Leopold and Land Health" (Ph.D. diss. University of Illinois at Urbana-Champaign, 2004; forthcoming from Island Press in 2006), 411–53.

7. David Pimentel, Laura Westra, and Reed F. Noss, eds., *Ecological Integrity: Integrating Environment, Conservation, and Health* (Washington, D.C.: Island Press, 2000); Paul L. Angermeier and James R. Karr, "Biological Integrity versus Biological Diversity as Policy Directives," *BioScience* 44

(1994): 690–97; J. Baird Callicott, Larry B. Crowder, and Karen Mumford, "Current Normative Concepts in Conservation," *Conservation Biology* 13 (1999): 22–35.

8. According to one detailed compilation, undertaken in 1995 based on various sources appearing in the early 1990s, combined state and federal land ownership in the United States accounted for 39.8 percent of all land. The compilation attempted to exclude water areas, leases, and easements and treated Indian tribal lands as private. The states varied in percentages of federal and state land ownership from less than 2 percent (Rhode Island and Kansas) to 95.8 percent (Alaska). National Wilderness Institute, "State by State Government Land Ownership," *http://www.nwi.org/Maps/Land-Chart.html* (visited March 28, 2005).

9. I offer comments on the subject in *The Land We Share: Private Property and the Common Good* (Washington, D.C.: Island Press, 2003), 241–48.

10. Herman E. Daly and Joshua Farley, *Ecological Economics: Principles and Applications* (Washington, D.C.: Island Press, 2004), 198–200.

11. Joseph Sax, "Why America Has a Property Rights Movement," *University of Illinois Law Review* (2005): 513–20.

12. Freyfogle, *The Land We Share,* 230–38.

13. Ibid., 78–81; William J. Novak, *The People's Welfare: Law and Regulation in Nineteenth-Century America* (Chapel Hill: University of North Carolina Press, 1996), 19–50.

14. Freyfogle, *The Land We Share,* 167–78; William E. Odum, "Environmental Degradation and the Tyranny of Small Decisions," *BioScience* 32 (1982): 728–29; Alfred E. Kahn, "The Tyranny of Small Decisions: Market Failures, Imperfections, and the Limits of Economics," *Kyklos* 19 (1966): 23–47.

15. Gary K. Meffe et al., eds., *Ecosystems Management: Adaptive, Community-Based Conservation* (Washington, D.C.: Island

Press, 2002); Richard Haeuber, "Setting the Environmental Policy Agenda: The Case of Ecosystem Management," *Natural Resources Journal* 36 (1996): 1–27; R. Edward Grumbine, "What Is Ecosystem Management?" *Conservation Biology* 8 (1994): 27–36.

16. David Western and R. Michael Wright, *Natural Connections: Perspectives in Community-Based Conservation* (Washington, D.C.: Island Press, 1994); Eve Endicott, ed., *Land Conservation through Public/Private Partnerships* (Washington, D.C.: Island Press, 1993); DeWitt John, *Civic Environmentalism: Alternatives to Regulation in States and Communities* (Washington, D.C.: Congressional Quarterly, 1994).

17. David W. Orr, *The Last Refuge: Patriotism, Politics, and the Environment in an Age of Terror* (Washington, D.C.: Island Press, 2004), 61–62.

18. Robert D. Bullard, *Dumping in Dixie: Race, Class, and Environmental Quality,* 3rd ed. (Boulder: Westview Press, 2000).

19. For instance, Gregg Easterbrook, *A Moment on the Earth: The Coming Age of Environmental Optimism* (New York: Viking, 1985), 317–33.

20. For instance, Thomas W. Merrill, "Private Property and the Politics of Environmental Protection," *Harvard Journal of Law and Public Policy* 28 (2004): 69–80 ("Just as private property generates more wealth, additional wealth generates more environmental protections"). For Merrill, politically active homeowners, defending the values of their private property, can play a role in bringing about environmental improvement, but environmental groups apparently do not nor do citizens who are guided by motives other than protecting the market values of their private property.

21. Ted Steinberg, *Down to Earth: Nature's Role in American History* (New York: Oxford University Press, 2002); John Opie, *Nature's Nation: An Environmental History of the United States* (Fort Worth: Harcourt Brace, 1998).

22. In contrast to the presumptions of conservation opponents and free market advocates are the findings of historians such as Samuel Hays. Samuel P. Hays, *Beauty, Health, and Permanence: Environmental Politics in the United States, 1955–1985* (Cambridge: Cambridge University Press, 1987); *Explorations in Environmental History* (Pittsburgh: University of Pittsburgh Press, 1998); *A History of Environmental Politics since 1945.* Journalistic histories of the environmental movement, though less reliable, also recount a far different story of environmental change and how it takes place. Philip Shabecoff, *A Fierce Green Fire: The American Environmental Movement* (New York: Hill and Wang, 1993); Robert Gottleib, *Forcing the Spring: The Transformation of the American Environmental Movement* (Washington, D.C.: Island Press, 1993). Figuring in the accounts of historians—and missing from the accounts of free market advocates—is the story of the concerted environmental opposition. Hays, *A History of Environmental Politics since 1945,* 109–21 ("By the 1990s it had become clear that the anti-environmental movement was a permanent feature of the landscape of public affairs"), 119.

23. A careful study of citizen engagement is Adam Rome, *The Bulldozer in the Countryside: Suburban Sprawl and the Rise of American Environmentalism* (Cambridge: Cambridge University Press, 2001).

24. Useful sources include Theodore Steinberg, *Acts of God: The Unnatural History of Natural Disasters in America* (New York: Oxford University Press, 2000); Donald Worster, *Dust Bowl: The Southern Plains in the 1930s* (New York: Oxford University Press, 1979); John McPhee, *The Control of Nature* (New York: Farrar, Straus and Giroux, 1989).

25. My ideas in this and the next several paragraphs have been much informed by Andrew Delbanco, *The Real American Dream: A Meditation on Hope* (Cambridge: Harvard University Press, 1999). I have also been aided by the writings of David

Ehrenfeld and David Orr discussed in entries 4 and 8, respec-
tively, in "Conservation's Central Readings: A Bibliographic
Essay."

26. Ibid., 70–80.
27. Ibid., 107.
28. Ibid., 111–18.

Index

Environmental goals. *See* Conservation goals

Environmental law. *See* Environmental scholarship

Environmental lawyer, 76

Environmental movement. *See* Conservation movement

Environmental problems: cultural flaws and, 17; Dust Bowl, 130–131; economic growth and, 203–204, 214; history of, 73–75; market forces in, 31–32, 35–38; natural disasters and, 204–205; private property and, 41, 191, 192, 203; schools of scholarship on, 68–70

Environmental progress: economic growth and, 201–204; market-oriented critics of, 200–201; national commitment to, 212–218; schools of scholarship on, 73–75; social norms and, 204

Environmental scholarship: on background issues, 78–80; central readings, 219–254; comparison to fiction writing, 52–54, 55, 81–82; complexity of, 79; on environmental problems, 68–70;

on environmental progress, 73–75; on goals, 72–73, 81; on human nature, 61–64; on human place in nature, 64–66; on knowledge-based decisionmaking, 66–68; motives and perceptions of, 54–55; schools of, 55–61; shift from value-driven approach, 76–77; spatial and temporal scales of analysis, 70–72; vision of society, 75; weakness of, 77–78. *See also* Tend-the-garden thinking; *specific names*

Equality ideal, conservation and, 41–43

Essential Agrarian Reader, The: The Future of Culture, Community, and Land (Wirzba), 229

Exotic species, 69, 156

Explorations in Environmental History (Hays), 232

Farley, Joshua, 253

"Farmer as a Conservationist, The" (Leopold), 86–94, 174–175

Farming in Nature's Image: An Ecological Approach to Agriculture (Soule and Piper), 246

Hays, Samuel P., 232, 267n2

Heritage Foundation, 84

History of Environmental Politics since 1945, A (Hays), 232

House of Life, The: Rachel Carson at Work (Brooks), 238

Howard, Albert, 30

Human-land bond, Leopold on, 88–90

Human nature, 61–64

Human needs, 45–46, 124, 136, 146–148, 175, 176

Human place in nature, 64–66, 145

Human utility, land management for, 146–148, 160–161

Hydrologic modification, 69

Income inequality, 197–198

In Defense of the Land Ethic (Callicott), 224

Individualism: in American culture, 65–66, 205–206; Berry on, 48; Leopold on, 48; responsible, 217–218; self-centered, 16–17. *See also* Libertarians

Individual liberty, 2, 39, 56, 155, 193, 217

International Union for the Conservation of Nature, 116

Intrinsic value of nature, 151–152

Jackson, Wes, 80, 116, 117, 245–246

"January Thaw" (Leopold), 220–221

Jayber Crow (Berry), 228

"Jilting of Granny Weatherall, The" (Porter), 52–53, 81

Job losses and gains, 137–138, 139, 141

Jordan, William, 171, 172

Keeping Afloat in the Age of Technology (Ehrenfeld), 234–235

Kline, David, 80

Knowledge-based decision-making, 66–68, 153–154, 193–194

Land community: Berry on, 30, 33, 34; Leopold on, 19–20, 45

Land community advocates: beliefs and approach of, 59–61; on environmental problems, 69–70; on environmental progress,

tion of, 33–34; ecological orientation of, 88–90; "The Farmer as a Conservationist," 86–94, 108–109, 174–175; on individualism, 48; influence of, 131–132, 133; on land-as-community, 19–20, 45; land ethic of, 18, 23; land health goal of, 20–23, 93–94, 128, 163–164, 182, 260n15; on land ownership, 25–26; on land-uses, 91–92; on roadless areas, 136; *Sand County Almanac*, 18, 20, 87, 220–223; on skilled landowner, 90–91

Leopold, Luna B., 224

Liberalism, conservation movement and, 6–8, 47–49

Libertarians, 40; beliefs and approach of, 55, 56; on conservation goals, 72; on environmental problems, 68; on human nature, 62, 63; spatial scale of analysis, 70–71

Liberty, individual, 2, 39, 51, 56, 155, 193, 217

Limerick, Patricia, 80

Lincoln, Abraham, 208, 209

Local communities: collective action by, 190–193; economy of, 32–33; land health and, 30, 33, 34; land-use wisdom in, 31; political divisions and, 15, 35

Logsdon, Gene, 80

MacKaye, Benton, 129

Manes, Christopher, 241

Manning, Richard, 80

Market forces, 31–32, 35–38, 50, 65, 148, 252–253. *See also* Free market fixers

Market-oriented view of environmental progress, 200–201

Market prices, 127, 198, 199–200

McIsaac, Greg, 118

McKibben, Bill, 80

Meffe, Gary K., 251

Meine, Curt, 224

Mills, Stephanie, 80

Mindful Conservatism: Rethinking the Ideological and Educational Basis of an Ecologically Sustainable Future (Bowers), 235

Monkey Wrench Gang, The (Abbey), 238

Moral universe, 134

Morgenstern, Oskar, 127

Muir, John, 239

Multiple-use land management, 127–129

Mumford, Lewis, 80, 131